O. Eugene Pickett
Borne on a Wintry Wind

"My search for a sustaining faith . . . took many directions. But it was in grappling with uncertainty and ambiguity, with pain and loneliness and the mystery of death that I was to discover meaning and hope. . . . If salvation comes, it probably will be as a small wave of light borne into my darkness on a wintry wind."—O. Eugene Pickett

O. Eugene Pickett
Borne on a Wintry Wind

Tom Owen-Towle

Skinner House Books
Boston

Published by Skinner House Books, an imprint of the
Unitarian Universalist Association, 25 Beacon Street,
Boston, Massachusetts 02108-2800.

Printed in Canada.

Photos on pages ii, 3, 6, 31, and 50 are from the library of O. Eugene
Pickett. Photo on page 212 is from the library of Kathleen Montgomery.
Portrait on page ii is by Robert Alexander Anderson.

10 9 8 7 6 5 4 3 2 1
99 98 97 96

Owen-Towle, Tom.
    O. Eugene Pickett : borne on a wintry wind : fourth president of
the Unitarian Universalist Association / Tom Owen-Towle.
        p.   cm.
    ISBN 1-55896-344-8 (alk. paper)
    1. Pickett, O. Eugene (Oliver Eugene), 1925- . 2. Unitarian
Universalist Association—Presidents—Biography. 3. Unitarian
Universalist Association—History. 4. Unitarian Universalists—
United States—Biography. I. Title.
BX9869.P53094   1996
289.1'092—dc20   96-7485
[B]   CIP

To Helen and Carolyn,
our beloved partners
who unfailingly cheer, nudge, and console us.

Contents

Preface

During the stretch of time my wife Carolyn was ardently pursuing the presidency of the Unitarian Universalist Association, I spent countless discretionary hours poring over twentieth-century denominational literature on Unitarian and Unitarian Universalist Association presidents, anticipating that such research would furnish useful knowledge in case she won the election.

A lover of biography since early childhood, I enjoyed sleuthing for relevant anecdotes and insights in the lives and writings of our religious executives. I started by revisiting *Pilot of a Liberal Faith: Samuel Atkins Eliot*, written by Arthur Cushman McGiffert, Jr., in 1976. Eliot, president of the American Unitarian Association (AUA) from 1900 to 1927, was known as a wise and contagiously buoyant leader who was affectionately called our "Miterless Bishop."

I then navigated the biography *Louis Cornish: Interpreter of Life*, an out-of-print volume that I fell upon years ago in a musty corner of our church library. Cornish served as president of the AUA from 1927 to 1937, and his journey was retold by his devoted wife, Frances E. F. Cornish.

I proceeded chronologically to engage *Frederick May Eliot: An Anthology*, edited by Alfred P. Stiernotte. The essays, including an impressive memorial address delivered by Wallace

Robbins, disclose the person of Eliot, AUA president from 1937 to 1957.

25 Beacon Street and Other Recollections by Dana McLean Greeley was the next stop along my archival quest. Greeley, a fifth-generation Unitarian, served as AUA president from 1958 to 1961 when he became the chief spiritual officer of the merged UUA, defeating William Rice by a vote of 1,135 to 980. Greeley's autobiography conveys his presidential aspirations and accomplishments through the lens of irrepressible optimism.

Robert Nelson West's years were anguished ones for the denomination. This complicated era was reviewed by West in his 1975 Minns' Lecture. Paul N. Carnes's time in office (1977 to 1979) was cut short by his untimely death to cancer. Although his presidential tenure had barely commenced, Carnes's wisdom remains available through published sermons and his book of prayers and invocations, *Longing of the Heart.*

William F. Schulz summarized his years at the UUA in his article, "Fifteen at 25," in the May/June 1993 issue of the *World* magazine. Bill's book, *Finding Time and Other Delicacies,* also manifests his trenchant thought and elegant expression.

The majority of Unitarian and Unitarian Universalist presidents since 1900 have had either their memoirs, prayers, addresses, or essays published. Although the parish ministry and presidential administration of O. Eugene Pickett stand among the most illustrious in our associational history, his story might well have gone untold, for he is neither publicly nor personally ambitious. Modifying Ralph Waldo

Emerson's claim that "there is properly no history, only biography," the thesis of *O. Eugene Pickett* is that through exploration of our religious leaders' lives, both the historical record and the theological perspective of our Unitarian Universalist movement are elucidated.

My tour of twentieth-century denominational drama made it evident to me that Pickett's biography would enhance the treasure trove of our shared "living tradition." Consequently, Carolyn and I invited the Picketts to our San Diego home in the spring of 1993 for a last-minute campaign strategy session and for my surprise proposal as well.

After we had finished dinner one evening, I cautiously posed the following question: "Gene, I have come to the conclusion that there should be a biography composed about your personal life, ministerial career, and presidential service, and, furthermore, with your support and collaboration, I would like to be the one to write it! What do you think?"

Stunned silence filled our living room, followed by Gene's terse reply: "Well, there's not enough material there!" Helen countered with her own proud and tearful response: "What a good idea! I wondered who might tell Gene's story. It's a story that should be told!" I persisted: "No rush, Gene. Think it over and after the election, we'll sit down again and see how you feel."

After General Assembly in Charlotte, North Carolina, we had our summit meeting as planned, and Gene gave a tentative green light. Only in August, when the initial package of sermons, addresses, and news clippings arrived in San Diego, did I sense that Pickett was releasing the brakes somewhat, enabling us to drive ahead.

Naturally, I had my share of anxieties about the delicate task of holding another's precious life in my hands, and more than once I have had to probe deep beneath Gene's fortified armor to mine the ore of his interior life. Furthermore, I have made no pretense to be an academic historian or to write a critical analysis. My mission has been solely to serve as a sympathetic yet truthful chronicler aspiring to reveal the intimate touches and presidential evolution of Eugene Pickett.

Yet, never once did I question the value of this venture or the worthiness of my subject. Despite Pickett's protestations to the contrary, there has proven no paucity of interesting life story to explore; and Gene, Helen, and I, working in concert, have generated abundant trust, respect, and affection. Alone, I *couldn't* have managed this formidable project; alone, Helen *shouldn't* have done it; and alone, Gene *wouldn't* have pursued it.

And truly this project was not accomplished alone. I am deeply indebted to the collaborative efforts of UUA staff members Judith Frediani and Brenda Wong for shepherding this project along.

Gene Pickett is a private, genuinely humble, even self-effacing, person, yet it is precisely the tales of the modest, unlikely leaders among us that need to be told. History is surfeited with biographies of larger-than-life prophets and bold, summery pioneers.

After our staunch Unitarian Universalist institutionalists leave office, they are often lightly regarded, if not forgotten, despite the critical foundations they have laid. As distinguished historian Conrad Wright observes in *Walking Together:*

"Of course the liberal tradition in religion has not been pure and unadulterated individualism. There have always been counter-currents and eddies; some religious liberals have criticized the excesses of individualism and stressed the value, significance and requirements of religious community. We have had Henry Ware, Jr., as well as Channing; we have had Frederick Henry Hedge as well as Emerson; we have had Henry Whitney Bellows as well as Octavious Brooks Frothingham. But we have seldom listened to these voices for long. We have not named churches for Bellows, who believed that churches are important; we name them for Emerson, who thought them superfluous."

Wright continues: "Usually, we limit ourselves to Emerson as the representative of spiritual religion and Theodore Parker as a voice of social reform. We overlook a whole range of other kinds of excellence. . . . No one of these can contribute all we need; they complement each other. It seems especially important to recover the role models appropriate for those who must take responsibility for the health of religious institutions, whether local or denominational."

Wright praises the importance of associational pillars like Pickett, whose steady yet undramatic leadership may be downplayed in history. Although we revel in the names of the stalwart individualists in our heritage, we identify more closely with our less flamboyant trailblazers and reliable community-builders. Pickett was singularly effective as our president in large measure because he was an unpretentious and vulnerable man, yet one with immense determination, striking decency, and political acumen. We can relate to and respect such authenticity of character.

In a religious heritage known for its upbeat, "onward and upward forever" worldview, Gene Pickett's self-professed "wintry spirituality" presents a countervailing current. The durable values and meanings of his faith journey have emerged from the depths of personal loneliness, pain, and uncertainty. His is a well-reasoned and weathered theology of adversity.

I have aspired to relate Eugene Pickett's saga straightforwardly, without artifice or unbecoming splendor, the way he has lived his life.

Tom Owen-Towle

Foreword

Tom Owen-Towle's portrait of Gene Pickett is nothing so much as a morality tale, albeit a morality tale of the most unlikely sort, one where hard work and authenticity and sheer tenacity prevail. It's a kind of modern day *Pilgrim's Progress* where, after exhilarating adventures and wrenching pain, the protagonist emerges with humor and maturity. And, of course, it's not really the story of just Gene at all. It's the story of a marriage, a ministry, and courage, told with more honesty than is usual.

I met Gene Pickett in the mid-sixties. He was the quirky and energetic minister of a fast-growing church that I attended from time to time. I remember, though I think he does not, that the first time I talked to him I demanded that he defend organized religion. He blanched.

For years I was a drop-in at what was called "Cliff Valley," the Unitarian Universalist Congregation of Atlanta, and by then the largest congregation in the Association. The energy there was astounding. It was rare for there to be an evening when the building wasn't ablaze with light and with hundreds of people—going to classes, workshops, and committee meetings, attending plays and lectures—and then often going out for coffee or a drink and more conversation. On Sunday the good-sized sanctuary was overflowing; you sat in the aisles or stood in the back if you got there late for the second service. It was heady stuff.

On Sundays after the services, people stood in clusters and argued and plotted, laughed and cried. And, oh my, how they criticized the sermons. How I criticized them! We wanted the minister to be more sophisticated, more glamorous, more dynamic. Today, more than twenty years later, I note that I remember parts of almost every sermon I heard him preach.

I joined finally, inevitably, but barely knew Gene. It was a church where you didn't need to know the minister, where volunteers had real power and access to it was easy, a church where I was nudged and encouraged and sometimes pushed into leadership roles. I remember only one first-hand contact with Gene. I was the newly appointed chair of the adult education committee. He called me into his office and suggested that I organize a day-long seminar designed to educate the community about gay and lesbian issues, an event to signal that homosexuals were welcome at the church. I thought the request odd and, pulling myself up (I was a very young thirty year old), advised him that doing so would be politically dangerous and, besides, there really *weren't* any gays or lesbians in the church. "Perhaps," he said, "but nevertheless . . ." In all the years since, Gene has never once reminded me of this.

Time passed. Gene left the church. In the winter of 1983 I found myself in his handsome office on Beacon Hill, overlooking the Boston Common. He was by then the president of the Unitarian Universalist Association. I was there to be interviewed for the job that ultimately brought me to Boston as a development officer. The interview was disconcerting—until I realized that he wasn't interviewing me at all. He was trying to help me decide if taking the job would be good for me.

In the years since then, Gene and Helen have become close friends of mine. I have dropped in at their various homes with impunity. We have taken innumerable walks and vacationed together. We often celebrate birthdays and holidays in one another's company. For years, when Gene was minister of the Church of the Larger Fellowship, we ate together every Friday night—same restaurant, same table—before the Picketts departed for their house on Cape Cod.

So I have known Gene mostly in the good times. He talks of years, whole decades, when he woke almost every night, obsessing and anguished. He tells me that now he wakes in the middle of the night to survey his current interests, smiles, often as not, and goes back to sleep. He and Helen talk of the hard years in their marriage—Helen, given a chance, will still rail—but I see the way they look at one another and how deeply content they are in each other's company. He talks of how hard ministry was for him, and how sometimes brutal the politics of the UUA—but I know that finally he knows what a success he was, and that he is both loved *and* respected in a profession to which he has given his life.

Gene talks about having a wintry personality and I suppose that is so. But I know him as the person who is always planning the next picnic and the next meal and the next political plot, the next garden and the next vacation and what book to take with him. He is tanned and he smiles easily. He forgets nothing but forgives readily. Perhaps it has been, as my mother used to say, more good luck than good management that he found the right spouse and the right therapist and the right profession. Or perhaps it was grace. In any case, it is good to know that life can come to this.

Kathleen Montgomery
Executive Vice President
Unitarian Universalist Association

A Maryland Country Childhood

"We can never tell what is in store for us."

HARRY S. TRUMAN

Family Roots

"From my childhood in rural Maryland, I recall vividly and with deep satisfaction the annual securing of home and hearth against the coming winter. We filled burlap bags with dried leaves and placed them in the cellar window wells for protection against the winds of winter. We filled the woodshed with split logs to feed the cook stove that would burn constantly until spring.

"In the backyard, under the gray sky, we stirred the apples in the large copper kettle until they became a rich brown butter. The pig we had fed and nurtured through the spring and summer was butchered and smoked and stored.

"And presiding over all these autumn rituals was my mother, a woman of independent spirit, provident by nature, ever protective of the family's well-being. These memories of autumn in my childhood have always brought feelings of comfort and closeness, but also feelings of melancholy and loneliness." —O. Eugene Pickett

Winfield, Maryland, had a population of perhaps 200 people when Oliver Burdette Pickett drove his horse and buggy fifteen miles to court Cora Ellen Danner. This rural village thirty miles from Baltimore boasted little more than a general store, a garage, an elementary school, and surrounding farms. The Picketts dealt in farm implements and repairs, and the Danners were dairy cattle farmers of German descent.

Cora and Ollie were nineteen and twenty-one years old when they married in 1911. Ollie had completed eleven years of schooling and pursued no further education. Cora attended two years of a business college where she learned shorthand. Cora, herself the youngest of thirteen children, joined the sizable Pickett clan when the couple set up a household in Winfield. Later, Cora's mother bought the Pickett home for her daughter for between six and seven thousand dollars and came to live with them. Cora took good care of Grandmother Danner for eight years, until her death in 1932.

Cora and Oliver had three boys. Marcus, born in 1913, was the oldest, and Harry arrived about eighteen months later. Oliver Eugene Pickett was born September 18, 1925. He was named after his father and the poet, Eugene Field. Eugene, as he was always called by his family, looked up to his older brothers and wished they would be his champions, but rather, they often picked on him. Once, in great anger, he chased one of his brothers through the house with a kitchen knife, but instead of hurting him, Eugene fell through a glass door and badly cut his own arm: a painful lesson in the possible ramifications of aggressive behavior.

Eugene's life was essentially that of an only child. He never shared a close relationship with either of his brothers due to differences in age and temperament. Of the two older siblings he spent more time with Harry, who was well liked in the larger community and took an interest in his young brother.

Eugene's Aunt Edna, who as a teenager raised her four younger brothers, including Ollie, married the town funeral director and lived next door to the Pickett family. Although Cora grew to feel competitive with her sister-in-law, the fam-

The Pickett family home in Winfield, Maryland, circa 1920. Seated on the steps are (left) *grandfather Pickett and father Ollie.*

ily benefited from Uncle Cliff's status. A mortician held a prominent position in the community. The undertaker, along with the doctors and ministers, represented the cream of Winfield's professional crop. Eugene's brother Harry became an apprentice at the mortuary, and some of Eugene's most pleasant childhood memories include helping Harry prepare graves and place artificial grass over the mounds of dirt. In these adventures Eugene forged a tenuous bond with his brother and felt he was doing something helpful.

The early exposure to the undertaker's business gave Eugene an easy familiarity with death and its trappings. "My grandfather Pickett had made caskets himself, and growing up we had great fun as kids climbing in and out of those displayed in the garage."

In a profound sense, this early familiarity with funerals, caskets, and death prefigured Pickett's development of a wintry spirituality, what he would later refer to as "a lifelong love affair with death."

Ollie and Cora

Ollie was a shadowy figure during Eugene's formative years. Ollie's father had been largely absent in his son's upbringing, and Ollie continued the pattern with his own sons.

During the Great Depression, Ollie followed his father's footsteps into the farm implement and plumbing business. At one point, finances became desperate, the enterprise went bankrupt, and Ollie was without work. He had a brother in Philadelphia whose midlevel management position with the

Pennsylvania Railroad provided him with a nice home and considerable prosperity. Roland, considered the successful Pickett brother, procured Ollie a job at the railroad station as a dispatcher for taxi cabs. Ollie lived with his brother, returning to Winfield every couple of months to visit his family. Unfortunately, he earned little money and sent only a modest amount home.

When Eugene was in the fifth grade, his father came home from Philadelphia, having been fired for drinking on the job. Ollie obtained a new position as the janitor at his son's school, primarily because of Cora's connections with the PTA and the recommendation of the teachers who boarded with them. Ollie continued to drink heavily as custodian, however, and Eugene often had to cover for him by sweeping the floors and stoking the furnace. This was an embarrassing and painful period.

Eugene's father could be kind and protective. Although Pickett would later write that "there just wasn't much of a basis for connecting meaningfully," he also described Ollie as "a mild-mannered man, intelligent and thoughtful" when he wasn't drinking. He loved to dress up in masquerade outfits. If there was anyone who had a sense of playfulness in the entire Pickett tribe it was Ollie. Lamentably, he was rebuked at such times of fun-filled zaniness by a wife who felt that the father's role was to be a provider not a clown.

Nonetheless, whenever there was money, Ollie would lavish gifts upon the family, both because of the pleasure it brought him and as a compensation for being an inadequate wage-earner and irregular presence. Ollie was not adept at showing either physical or emotional affection and was absent most of the time. The best way he knew to care for Eugene was through gift-giving outbursts. Ollie was a volatile contradiction: a source of anguish and humiliation yet often a generous and caring father. Pickett would later describe his family situation as one that "compounded a basic sense of insecurity, restlessness, and uncertainty that I have never overcome."

Cora was the dominant force in the family and clearly the parent with whom all the boys bonded, especially Eugene, or "little Eugene," as he was both affectionately and somewhat condescendingly called by family members. He was the apple of his mother's eye and her major source of emotional support, since the older boys were otherwise occupied and Ollie was away looking for work.

Eugene at age 10 with his mother Cora.

With Ollie's uncertain employment, Eugene's mother shouldered the primary responsibility for raising the family. Cora was an assertive and enterprising woman, but the financial strain was great. She worked as a notary public and rented rooms to teachers in the public school as an additional means of earning money. She was a handsome, well-groomed, and dignified woman, who possessed high standards about her own children's appearance. The boys never went hungry and were dressed respectably, although usually in second-hand clothes.

When the Great Depression struck, Pickett's mother, blessed with strong survival instincts, was concerned about Marcus's job prospects. Cora was quite active in Republican politics in Winfield and served on the State Central Committee. Marcus had been driving trucks, but Cora was able to capitalize on her political connections and secure him a state job, with which he remained his entire working career, rising to the post of Chief Examiner for the Commission of Motor Vehicles. Cora's political knack was exceptional and stood her in good stead throughout an arduous, trying life. It was a proclivity and talent that her son Eugene inherited.

Because Cora and Eugene were alone together throughout his early growing up years, they developed a symbiotic relationship. Cora survived these hard years in part by leaning on "little Eugene" for inappropriate nurturance. Later in life, Pickett would recall that "Mom was not a very affectionate person, but even through my seminary education, I always felt responsible for her."

Ollie and Cora grew physically apart and emotionally distant from one another. Their marriage, although never reaching the point of divorce, was unsatisfactory. Cora never kicked her husband out of the house, but there was a good deal of quarreling. One time Ollie even grabbed a gun and, threatening to shoot, frightened Cora and Eugene into locking themselves into the bedroom as Ollie remained outside. Luckily, this storm passed without actually escalating into physical harm.

Cora became increasingly discouraged with Ollie's alcoholism and resultant inability to be a consistent provider. She would constantly scold her husband. Later, as Pickett gained perspective through therapy on his family's pathologic interactions, he realized that his mother felt compelled to shame his father because she considered him a failure. This dysfunctional pattern took its toll on Ollie, Cora, and Eugene.

Pickett remembers a photograph of his parents in their early married years that showed two good-looking adults who seemed to exude happiness. Later, when Cora was bemoaning what a poor marriage hers had been, he remarked, "Well, Mom, were there any happy days in the beginning?" And she admitted that there had been some. But because Eugene came along twelve years later, sadly, he missed out on whatever good relations his parents might once have had.

An Outsider

Gene remembers his childhood as a lonely one. His brothers were considerably older and had different interests; his father was away; his mother was self-absorbed and needy; there were few children his age in the village. He felt alone;

he was alone. His closest childhood friend was a cousin about five years older. Mary Jane, Aunt Edna's daughter, who lived next door, and Pickett have remained close throughout their lives, forging an enduring family tie.

Mary Jane recalls their shared childhood: "We were very close to one another as children. When Eugene's mother didn't have a snack on hand, he came to our home for one—especially devil's food cake. We went to a very small school. Before he was old enough to attend school, he went with me in the mornings. When he started first grade, Eugene cried every day for the first two weeks. After that, he became a good, hardworking student through all his years.

"Eugene was always trying something new. One summer it was painting. We went to Ocean City, Maryland, for a few days, and he took his easel, canvas, and paints. Each day he went on the beach and painted. The artwork didn't amount to much, but he did get a lot of attention.

"I guess the last big thing we did together was learn to drive. His father had an old Ford, and we took it to the school grounds to practice. He got his license first and then took me to get mine.

"We always had a lot of fun, and I don't remember ever having an argument with him. He was a happy-go-lucky youngster and everyone liked him."

Eugene was well-liked by his peers, even if thought something of a "nerd" because of his passion for reading. He recalls that he "gained a sense of survival through reading books and would lose myself in fantasies derived from books by Somerset Maugham and Thomas Wolfe." Eugene was also considered strange because his mother dressed him in knickers when all the other boys were wearing long pants. They were his brother's castoffs and were all the family could afford, yet Cora never fully appreciated how awkward and out of place Eugene felt wearing them. He joined the 4-H club, but again felt alien in the group. Because he did not live on a farm and have access to livestock, he decided to raise pheasants. None of his peers had ever dreamed of raising pheasants!

Eugene related better to adults in the neighborhood than to his peers. He didn't engage in athletics because he was too near-sighted to see balls coming to him. Instead, he loved clerking at the general store even while he was still in grade school. Although he babysat occasionally, he felt more comfortable around older people.

At school Eugene was something of a teacher's pet. Unfortunately, for years no one realized that he needed glasses, so he had difficulty seeing blackboards and other objects at a distance. Eugene never complained, but tried to please his teachers in the same way that he would placate his mother. His first-grade teacher was Leona Gaver, a young woman in her first year of teaching. Eugene responded well and became a good student, which was fortunate, because before long, Leona married Marcus and became Eugene's sister-in-law. They were to become and remain good friends throughout her life.

During his ministerial career, Gene frequently preached on the theme of loneliness because it was a perpetual dimension of his own life. Preaching in Atlanta in 1972, he phrased it this way: "Looking back, I realize how lonely were the years of my growing up. I cannot recall anyone that I could share significant experiences or thoughts with, that I could confide my doubts and yearnings to, that I felt that I could trust with my deepest feelings. In high school I discovered Thomas Wolfe, and I remember that just the titles of his books like *Look Homeward Angel* and *You Can't Go Home Again* could stir my feelings of loneliness to the point of tears. Wolfe comforted me by pointing out that my loneliness could be potentially creative as well as potentially crippling."

Unquestionably, in his growing-up years, Eugene considered himself an outsider, different from both his Winfield neighbors and his own family members. He turned inward. He read. He daydreamed. And he realized during his high school years that the only way out of this rural isolation was through the doorway of college.

A Pious Methodist

Eugene was not involved in organizations such as the YMCA or Boy Scouts, but he was very active at Ebenezer church, the local, pietistic Methodist church that doubled as the hub of social life in the community. Ollie rarely attended church, but Cora was active, especially in the women's group. The church was part of family life in many ways. Eugene remembers one young Methodist minister coming over to their house to smoke and drink with his older brother Harry (with the blinds pulled, naturally).

Eugene earned seven years of perfect Sunday school attendance for which he was given bar pins. At the tender age of fourteen, he served as Sunday school superintendent, with responsibility for keeping the attendance rolls for classes, making sure that there were enough crayons on the tables, and announcing the closing hymn. This "adult-child" role was Eugene's way of gaining acceptance and self-esteem as well as displaying an incipient gift for leadership. But at that time, he did not feel "called" to any church work, let alone parish ministry.

Eugene not only suffered from father-hunger, but also felt an absence of effective male mentors in his youth. All of his role models were women, especially school teachers. The closest male exemplar was Reverend Isaacs, a Methodist minister and director of the local orphanage. Eugene would go home with the Isaacs's son, Reid, one of only two close friends, and sit down to a dinner prefaced with a prayer and served with style. The Isaacs seemed to do all the right things that Eugene missed in his own family. Reverend Isaacs seemed to be a model father who planted the seeds of a budding social conscience in Eugene, whose family were conservative Republicans and also racially prejudiced. The Isaacs family opened the doors of his mind and heart.

Eugene was a devout youth who accepted uncritically the Methodist orthodoxy. He would become emotionally involved simply enacting characters in the Old Testament stories. At this time, his God was hard-nosed, granting reward's only to those who were diligent and productive, and punishing those who were lazy or who misbehaved.

Yearning to Leave Winfield

In high school Eugene was a good student, well-liked by teachers and popular with peers. He served on the student council and was elected president of his senior class. Only a handful of the fifty graduates would go on to college, and Eugene was one of them. Being a well-behaved, high-achieving youth was the way he chose to gain recognition and acceptance. He was even designated "most likely to succeed" in his high school yearbook. His biggest disappointment of his high school career was not being able to play the narrator in Thornton Wilder's play, *Our Town*, because he became ill. Fortunately, he has recreated that role over and over again in dramatic presentations performed in his churches. One of Pickett's favorite lines has the narrator speaking: "We all know that nature's interested in quantity; but I think she's interested in quality, too—that's why I'm in the ministry!"

Eugene's social skills were underdeveloped. He was awkward around girls because he was shy and didn't know what to say or do. He dated for dances, but the Picketts lived fifteen miles from the nearest town, and he didn't have a car. Youth living in the country in those days were generally isolated from one another.

During summers Eugene hoed corn and worked in a woolen mill, both jobs he loathed. One advantage of the mill job, however, was that he could obtain wool to make suits and keep himself well dressed.

The one job Eugene enjoyed more than any other was clerking in a general merchandise store where two older men took a liking to him. Their influence was not necessarily positive, but it was enlightening. They would take Eugene with them to Baltimore where they operated an open stall market selling chickens, eggs, and produce. Eugene worked alongside them on Saturdays and considered it great sport. These men were hard drinkers and they exposed little Eugene to the wider, wilder world.

Eugene wanted to get out of Winfield. There was no one in this rural village with whom to discuss the weightier matters of life like vocation, relationships, and meaning. Seeking to broaden his horizons, he applied as a day student to the University of Baltimore to study accounting. He thought business school might be the right fit, since he had labored happily for several years in the general store.

But again, Cora's determination and resources prevailed. Through her active participation in the local Methodist church, she discovered that the American University in Washington, DC, was a Methodist school that offered scholarships. Thanks to his mother's advocacy, Eugene received a stipend that supplemented the financial resources he had accumulated through working.

Eugene's first year in college was inordinately difficult. He was at a considerable academic disadvantage, having attended a high school with no science lab and inadequate language studies. Furthermore, because he was only sixteen years old, he was socially and intellectually unprepared for the rigors of college life. Eugene joined a fraternity where for the first time he bonded with a social group, although it happened to be a fraternity comprising of fairly sanctimonious types. He became the scribe and was duly acknowledged for his leadership abilities, so that by the end of the year, he had made a successful adjustment to college.

The Circuitous Path to the Ministry

"To believe in something not yet proved, and to underwrite it with our lives . . . to find the delicate equilibrium between dream and reality; the hour when faith in the future becomes knowledge of the past; to lay down one's power for others in need; to shake off the old ordeal and get ready for the new; to question, knowing that never can the full answer be found; to accept uncertainties quietly; to know that this is what life's journey is about."

LILLIAN SMITH, *THE JOURNEY*

Coming of Age in the Navy

In 1943, Pickett's second year of college, the United States had been at war for two years. He was due to be drafted, so he enlisted in order to have the choice of joining the Navy. He did not know enough at the time to become a conscientious objector, although he was one in spirit and temperament. He simply saw no way out of military conscription. Gene entered the military at the age of eighteen, a lonely and frightened young man. Emotionally, he barely survived the twelve weeks of boot camp.

During his three semesters at American University, Pickett had begun to lose his Methodism. The new and exciting exposure to philosophy and science was causing him to question orthodox Protestantism. However, when he first entered the Navy, he was so frightened that he returned to his Methodist beliefs, pleading to God for help and comfort. But he received no answers from above or below, from God or human.

A particular incident led to growing disillusionment with conventional religion. When Gene attended a chapel service on the base, he and the other lesser ranked personnel were ordered to move out of the front pew so the officers could sit there. Gene was incensed by this display of entitlement, especially in church where he thought equality was valued. In fact, this keen sense of egalitarianism was to be a major thread throughout Pickett's career.

When Gene entered Navy Medical Corps school, he gained both confidence and meaningful relationships. He was befriended by a Marxist teacher from New York who introduced him to the radical social philosophy of Theodore Dreiser, James T. Farrell, and Leo Tolstoy and to such classics as *Crime and Punishment.* Gene could easily identify with the socially and economically disadvantaged people of the world, primarily through his own sense of being an outsider. Gene kept writing home for books on intellectually rigorous subjects, a request which completely baffled his Winfield kin.

Gene was flattered that his older male colleagues in the Navy were interested in engaging him in serious discussions. He also felt valued while using his practical nursing skills among the South Pacific wounded. In spite of the initial trauma of military training, his tour of duty matured him immensely. After three years in the Navy, Gene almost re-enlisted for the financial independence, freedom of movement, and intellectual stimulation he had enjoyed. He had clearly outgrown the folkways of Winfield.

While serving in the Navy, Gene also experienced a close personal loss. His brother Harry was tragically killed in a mine sweeper that sank off the Carolina coast during a hurricane. He was thirty years old and had left behind a pregnant wife. Harry was considered "missing in action" for a number of years before the Navy confirmed the death.

When Gene returned home, he was immediately entrapped once again in providing emotional support to his mother, who overwhelmed her son with a litany of her aches and pains. Pickett once remarked, "Although my mother was actually a very healthy woman until her later years, she wasn't well a day in her life." She lived to the age of ninety-six.

First Romance

When Gene returned to American University in 1946 he was twenty-one. He resumed his romantic involvement with a woman named Gladys who was fifteen years older than him and had once been married. They had met in the college library where she worked as the switchboard operator.

Gladys taught the impressionable Gene about the sophisticated life. The first time they went out drinking and ordered a cocktail, the waitress glanced at Gladys to see if it was all right for Gene to have a drink because he looked so young. Gladys was an all-consuming interest for some time, and when she and Gene came to visit Winfield, the family was shocked and distraught. If he was subliminally trying to rattle his family, he succeeded.

Upon returning to college, Gene had no interest in entering dormitory life again, so he took a room close to the campus in the home of a prim and proper older woman who happened to attend All Souls Unitarian Church, a fact he did not know at the time. Mary Crook rented rooms to a series of college students, primarily because she enjoyed their company, for she did not need the money. Mary became something of a mother figure to Gene. She lived in an attractive, spacious house; had never married; took care of the boarders for minimal rent; and showed considerable interest in whatever the students were reading, thinking, and doing. She treated them like members of the family, remembered their birthdays, and often sat in the living room engaging them in serious conversation. This extended family arrangement met both her needs and those of Gene. Unlike Gladys, Mary proved unthreatening to Gene's mother, although Cora would have relished such a comfortable domestic situation for herself.

Gene lived in Mary's home for the duration of his college career, and stayed in communication with her until she died. She even bequeathed some money to Pickett when she died, the only money he ever inherited.

Politics

After leaving military service, Pickett realized that his courses of study at American University needed direction, and he considered two career possibilities: working in government or teaching history and political science. Again, his mother's influence would come into play.

When Gene was taking political science courses at American University, one of his professors strongly recommended that the students attend a lecture by Glenn Taylor, Vice Presidential candidate with Henry Wallace on the Progressive Party ticket. So Gene went to hear Taylor at All Souls Unitarian Church and entered a Unitarian Church for the first time. He was intrigued.

In 1947, Gene was selected as one of four students to participate in the Washington Semester, a new program that American University and a half-dozen other liberal arts colleges were developing. Each college sent several students to the capitol for a semester to learn about government. They lived in their own dormitory and were assigned faculty advisors. At that time Joseph McCarthy was a new, almost reticent, Republican Senator. Cora, a member of the Republican State Committee, used her Maryland connections to arrange an internship for Gene in Senator McCarthy's office. Through her savvy and tenacity, Cora had helped another one of her sons find a position.

At the time, nobody could have predicted the later notoriety of this new legislator. Gene picked up McCarthy's laundry, counted his mail, and generally was a "go-fer" for the Senator's office. Ironically, years later in the Miami church where Gene chaired evening forums often featuring left-wing programs, he gave a review of the Beacon Press book entitled *McCarthy: The Man, the Senator, the Ism,* and denounced McCarthy's demagoguery. In the context of reviewing McCarthyism, Gene mentioned that he had worked in Senator McCarthy's office years before as a college student and that he knew that members of Congress paid serious attention to their mail.

The next morning Pickett received a telegram from McCarthy's office saying: "You did not work in my office. I have never met you. And I expect you to retract this. Notify all who heard you and report to me when accomplished. Signed: Senator Joseph McCarthy." Someone at the evening forum had reported everything happening at the Miami Unitarian Church to McCarthy's office overnight. Gene responded with a letter to McCarthy detailing his internship in the Senator's office, but heard no more from McCarthy's office. The whole exchange was rather chilling, because McCarthy was then at the height of his anti-Communist witch hunts.

Despite the narrowly conservative political and social views of his family, Gene's politics took a distinct turn to the left during his career at American University. If he had known then how repressive McCarthy's ideology would become, he would never have worked for him. Impressed with the socially liberal platform of the Progressive Party, Gene obtained a press card to attend their National Convention in Philadelphia. Wallace was defeated, but Gene became engrossed in the politics of that campaign. Although it never dawned on him that someday he would be a leader in a significant progressive organization, he had begun to reveal political proclivities of his own.

A Lark, Not a Call

In college, Gene had acquitted himsclf well in both political science and history, especially in projects like the Washington Semester practicum. He grew interested in pursuing graduate school but was unsure about a specialty. Around this time Gene began visiting All Souls Unitarian Church to hear the preaching of A. Powell Davies, a major ministerial presence in Washington, DC, during the 1940s. Gene was impressed with Davies and with the left-wing meetings at All Souls Unitarian Church, which were in stark contrast to the social conscience of the Methodist tradition that was more pietistic than progressive. Davies was a powerful preacher who resolutely addressed contemporary issues. He spoke from a manuscript and, even when he stumbled, parishioners remained glued to their seats, hanging onto his every word. Gene thought to himself: "If I could learn to read a sermon manuscript well, I, too, could preach!"

His pathway to seminary education took strange and unpredictable turns. Gene remembers drinking too much with fellow students one night, and two of them, including Pickett, declared their curiosity regarding the Unitarian ministry. Neither of them knew what theological education was really about, but Gene liked the fact that one of the Unitarian seminaries was at the University of Chicago. Captivated by the reputation of this academic complex, Pickett planned to explore seminary life, and if theological training didn't work out, he would simply switch to one of the other graduate schools in the university. Benefiting from the GI Bill, Gene felt financially free to take this course of action. In sum, Gene chose seminary more on a lark than because of a call.

So Pickett took his first step toward the Unitarian ministry by making an appointment with Davies. He was both excited and nervous as he strode into the office of this moral giant. Despite his high expectations, Gene was ushered in and out after only a 20-minute visit. Pickett felt disheartened by the brevity of their exchange, and once again, let down by a father-figure. He had learned little about either the ministry or theological training. Although Davies was noncommittal about Pickett's future, he at least agreed to write a letter.

Years later when Gene was serving the Unitarian parish in Richmond, Virginia, word filtered back to Davies that he had not paid adequate attention to Pickett. Faced with the fact that Gene had become a colleague right next door to him, Davies made amends by inviting the Picketts to a special ministerial gathering in the Greater Washington area and inviting Gene to preach at All Souls.

In looking back at the road that led him to be a minister, Pickett remembers most his uncle's funeral parlor: "Though I didn't realize it then, my own spiritual journey started in the funeral parlor of my uncle where I and other children played hide-and-seek amongst the empty caskets. My having grown up, in a sense, in a funeral home will someday make it possible, I suppose, to say of my life that it quite literally came full circle.

"The presence of death, the exposure to corpses, was commonplace to me as a child, and human limitation and mortality were natural and ever-present facts about existence.

But my orthodox Methodist upbringing regarded death quite differently; regarded it and all other aspects of life in fact as part of an intractable plan which allowed for no deviation, ambiguity, or questioning. What I took to be natural my elders' religion taught to be the gateway to possible terror.

"Later, when I became a Navy medical corpsman stationed in Jacksonville, Florida, during World War II, I learned first-hand the real terror of the dying. For Jacksonville was where the Navy shipped its living casualties from the South Pacific—young bodies burned and mangled, young men desperate to retrieve a vitality quickly ebbing. As I worked among these young men, weighed down by the assumption that I needed to provide them some theological encouragement about their dying, I realized that most of them were not worried about salvation. They simply needed me to hold their hands and let them feel I cared.

"That realization, coupled with my later collegiate encounter with the empirical tradition, prompted me to throw off orthodoxy and take on the kind of liberating religion I discovered at All Souls Unitarian Church in Washington, DC. Here was a faith which combined the passion of my early orthodox upbringing with the sensibilities of my new discoveries. What I found in Washington was a holistic religion, a faith for the whole person. The appeal of Unitarian Universalism for me has always been its holistic approach to life."

The Meadville Daze

"Heroes take journeys, confront dragons, and
discover the treasure of their true selves."

CAROL PEARSON

Confronting the Dragon

Gene took the train to Meadville/Lombard Theological
School in the fall of 1948, uncertain about who he was
and what he wanted to do, but gambling that seminary
might furnish the context to help answer these two burning questions.

There were between seventeen and twenty students at
Meadville/Lombard with six in Pickett's class: David Osborn,
Bob Kiefer, Hugo Leaming, Emil Gudmundson, John Wolf,
and Gene. When Gene arrived, he didn't know any students,
faculty, or ministers, except Davies who was on the Board of
Trustees.

Just as Gene had been unprepared for his first year in
college, he was unprepared for some of the challenges of
seminary life. He had little experience in public speaking
and writing and felt insecure in both areas. Gene had also
learned how to be a pious young man—pious in the ambigu-

ous sense of both harboring a social conscience and also being "too good to be true." The "sweet and gentle Jesus" of Gene's early Methodist training had stayed with him for years, but by the time he entered seminary Pickett was a thoroughgoing humanist, and he was even becoming anti-Christian. Yet, by the standards of fellow students, Gene was too pious, and they mocked him by taping pictures of a sentimentally drawn Jesus above his bed.

And, of course, his conflicted relationship with his mother followed him to Chicago. Up to this point Gene had endured his mother's need to control and rely on him. Now his frustrations and hurts began to cascade. Gene slowly asserted himself, breaking the fetters with his family. Cora could sense Gene's pulling away, so the resentments were reciprocated.

One of the reasons Gene was exploring the ministry was "to get myself sorted out." After about a year at seminary, he was not accomplishing that goal. Instead Gene was experiencing enormous uncertainty about his identity and where he was headed.

He had grown miserable, even suicidal, so it was utter desolation that drove him to seek counseling. He felt hopelessly entangled. His relationship with his mother was tormented and enervating. He readily discovered that going to seminary would not extricate him from his personal quagmire. Furthermore, Meadville wasn't the supportive, extended family he had anticipated and desired. Instead, seminary was a competitive environment that drove him deeper into depression. Therapy was his final hope. "If I hadn't gotten myself straightened out at this point, I would probably have committed suicide. I didn't try, but it was constantly in my thoughts. Therapy literally saved me!"

Wallace Robbins, president of Meadville/Lombard Theological School at this time, was anti-Freudian and opposed to most kinds of counseling, despite the fact that "perhaps half of the student body were sneaking away to receive therapy." There were no professors on campus who truly understood the emotional tribulations of the students or supported their need for therapeutic assistance.

In the Chicago School of Psychoanalysis, one could receive controlled analysis at a reduced cost because the services of students-in-training were employed. Gene applied for this program but was not accepted. He knew he needed help, so he started working at the Billings Hospital at the University of Chicago as a bookkeeper in the evenings to pay for psychoanalysis, which he received three times a week for three years.

Gene also held jobs during the day at Meadville, waiting on tables and serving as a proctor in the dorm. During the summers he employed his skills as a Navy medic to work as a private duty nurse. Gene was dogged in acquiring the funds necessary to take care of his anguished soul.

Gene's analyst was a woman of Austrian Jewish background, an orthodox Freudian, who felt that as soon as Gene was cured, he would discard the ministry business. She had Gene lie on the couch and engage in free association and in dream interpretation. Therapy revealed that Gene's psychic survival as a child had depended on keeping his interior life secret from his mother. It was a matter of self-protection. The boundaries between what was appropriately private, personal, and public grew unclear and generated anxiety in Gene about self-disclosure. It was hard for Gene to navigate between being naturally and appropriately a private person and being forced by early fear and shame to harbor secrets.

In addition to his need to disconnect from the smothering bond with his mother, Gene struggled with the "Impostor Syndrome," an emotional condition where one is obsessed by the thought: "If they only knew how inadequate I am, they would never believe in or respect me. . . ." This mind-set was related to the deep depression that he faced in therapy: "If they only knew how unworthy I really am."

Unable to overcome intensive self-criticism, impostors attribute their success to external events instead of taking credit for their own talents. They suffer from anxiety, depression, or embarrassment, convinced that their "fake fronts" have misled others, or that their self-perceived fraudulence will be uncovered. Gene's therapy revealed that the primary reason he had difficulty putting anything down on paper was the persistent fear of exposing himself to rejection, and proving himself unworthy in the eyes of others. Gene experienced a severe case of the impostor syndrome throughout his life both privately and publicly, as a father and husband as well as a minister and political leader.

The roots of this devitalizing syndrome are grounded in Gene's family history. His father was, in Gene's terms, "a pretty inadequate person." His mother did little to bolster her son's self-confidence as a child, nor did his brothers, except perhaps Harry before his life was cut short. Even when Gene would visit the Pickett clan as an adult, he was still perceived to be "little Eugene," the tag-along brother.

He was not regarded as a full-fledged adult by members of his family.

Overall, the psychoanalysis worked effectively because Gene was hungry and receptive. Unquestionably, this grueling emotional rehabilitation ultimately made Pickett a more mature, sensitive minister. As Thornton Wilder has perceptively noted: "In love's service, only the wounded can serve."

"To Save the World"

Pickett had enrolled at Meadville to clarify his identity. He also brought a pure yet unformed social conscience: "I simply wanted to do some good." His reflections on his reasons for entering the ministry illuminate some of his thinking at this time.

"My decision to enter the ministry was quite tentative and my motivation unclear. My reasons were both idealistic and selfish. I knew very little about either the ministry or Unitarianism. The statement I wrote as to why I wanted to go into the ministry had something to do with 'working with and helping people, wanting to make this a better world,' and I'm certain I must have mentioned something about peace and justice and brotherhood. In other words, I wanted to save the world.

"At one level I think I was being honest, but at a deeper and more significant level I was really saying I wanted to save *myself*. I was trying to cope with the most basic of questions: 'Why am I here?' 'What is the meaning of life and, most particularly, what is the meaning of *my* life?' My own search for meaning was a major struggle throughout my ministry. Perhaps it was the most basic struggle, for, unless we come to terms with this question in our own lives, it is difficult to be of much help to others in their search for meaning."

Years later, while looking back at his struggles with ministry, Pickett said, "Periodically, I have gone through the throes of deciding if I should leave the ministry—a not uncommon feeling among ministers I have known. My dissatisfaction did not come from wanting to do something else, but rather from feelings of insecurity as a person and inadequacy as a minister—from a realization that I could never accomplish what I thought I ought to accomplish. That I have been able to deal with and work through these ambivalent feelings, and that I have achieved a degree of success in the ministry and happiness in my life, I attribute, in large measure, to four years at Meadville/Lombard, three understanding congregations, two insightful psychiatrists, and a wife who refused to remain in a pear tree!"

Student Life

During Gene's first year in Chicago, the Chinese Communists ousted the Nationalists to Formosa. Consequently, a number of Nationalist students at the University of Chicago were left with no means of support. The university did not allow them to stay on campus, but since there were empty beds at his seminary, Gene mounted a campaign to find room for these ostracized Chinese students at Meadville. Some students were supportive of his plan, but the administration was opposed. This was one of many times in Pickett's life when he personally identified with the stranger, the underdog, the outsider. Gene was a reluctant, yet forthright radical in his social witness, deeply involved in challenges of conscience. He was gentle but steadfast in his efforts as a maturing social activist.

Gene was popular with the student body and was elected president during his third year. He was also a proctor that same year, hand-picked by school president Wallace Robbins to serve as a liaison between the students and the president. The proctor handled such logistical responsibilities as sending the linen to the laundry, locking doors at night, making announcements in the dining room, and putting proper notices on the bulletin board. This experience would stand

Pickett (standing) *waiting table in Meadville House dining room. Other students are:* (left to right) *Christopher Moore, Donald Thompson, Michip Akashi, a visitor, David Osborn, and John Wolf.*

Gene in good stead years later in his Atlanta church where there was never more than part-time custodial service, and, in an effort to keep the church appearance in alignment with his high standards, Gene did his share of vacuuming carpets and straightening chairs.

With extracurricular activities added to Gene's demanding work load and therapy schedule, there was not much time left over for studies. Gene was intelligent but certainly no scholar. He possessed neither an intellectual thirst for pure knowledge nor the personal discipline to stay focused on the academic program at Meadville. In fact, he was an average student academically because he was engrossed in so many other endeavors. As Gene remembers it, his fellow Meadville students in the early 1950s were all bright enough to get through seminary without much effort.

Pickett's most stimulating course proved to be "Religion and Personality" taught by Seward Hiltner. It emphasized Carl Rogers's nondirective approach to counseling, which stood in strong contrast to the directive psychoanalytic therapy that Gene was concurrently undergoing. This contrast furnished a lively and fruitful tension in his life, and he grew to appreciate the preeminent value of the Rogerian method for use in the parish ministry.

Gene was a rationalistic humanist, a theological stance that was considerably out of favor with Meadville faculty members such as James Luther Adams and President Wallace Robbins (both liberal Christians) and Bernard Meland, a process theologian. Pickett's theology was rough-hewn and unsophisticated, essentially a rebellious posture against the orthodoxy of his heritage. He was influenced by the psychological work of Erich Fromm, Karen Horney, and Rollo May more than by any systematic theologian. His thinking was shaped primarily by the actual details and challenges of daily life. He was profoundly enmeshed in his own personal development; formal theology played a secondary role.

Student Rebellion

Most of the seminary students, like Gene, were in their early to middle twenties. There was considerable student dissatisfaction with both the administration and the board. The students were upset with Robbins's position that they should focus exclusively on academics and not be involved in such luxuries as therapy or field work. Although other federated theological schools in the University of Chicago consortium required field work, Meadville discouraged it.

Students expressed other dissatisfactions, including the complaint that Robbins was prone to favoritism and that the admissions procedures were haphazard and arbitrary. Student concerns for improving the quality of life at the school were not taken seriously, and tension and animosity kept building until 1949 when the students decided formally to register their grievances. Professor James Luther Adams encouraged them to mount their modest resistance, yet when the rebellion escalated, Adams grew uneasy.

The students hired a prominent labor lawyer who advised them to write statements verifying all their grievances. They took their complaints, which made up a substantial volume, directly to the Board in a bold attempt to challenge the President of Meadville. When it arrived, everything blew wide open. Meadville's trustees, including A. Powell Davies, were furious with the students. Other copies of this document were to be ferreted out and destroyed immediately.

Frederick May Eliot, president of the American Unitarian Association, made a special trip to Meadville and threatened the students, saying that anyone who continued to defy authority in this manner would never get a church while he was president. Ironically, Gene had already been involved in negotiations with Joseph Barth, classmate and friend of Wallace Robbins, to go to Miami for a summer ministerial internship. Barth rose above the crisis and told Pickett, "Your rebellion doesn't make any difference to me. This battle is between you and Meadville. If you decide upon our ministerial post in Miami, come on down!"

This insurrection consumed the student body for Pickett's fourth and final year. He had stayed an additional academic year to continue his therapy while leading the resistance. Every Meadville student but two signed the bill of complaints. Only Carl Wennerstrom, a Unitarian graduate student at the Chicago Divinity School who later taught at Meadville/Lombard, and Dr. Leslie Pennington, who was the minister at First Unitarian Church in Chicago, supported the students. Robbins was especially angry at ring leader Pickett, who had been one of his personal favorites among the students. Robbins felt betrayed, and it wasn't until near the end of Robbins's life that the two of them achieved a degree of civility.

Leading this rebellion was a pivotal experience for Pickett: it furnished a golden opportunity for him to demonstrate courageous and empowering leadership. He proved to be a bold and insistent leader without being self-absorbed or flashy. Glitter plays on the surface of things and people; it dazzles while making one dizzy. Sparkle gives a reflected radiance, it has depth. The personality, and ensuing ministry, of Gene Pickett sparkled rather than dazzled.

Gene had entered seminary because he felt ministry was the craft of community-building and justice-making. Advocacy for student rights was a litmus test for answering this call. The rebellion also displayed Pickett's willingness to speak truth to power and to take brave risks with serious consequences. Gene describes this epoch of his student body presidency, like all of his leadership posts, with reserve, even self-deprecation, citing, "I guess I was the only one who would do it!" On the contrary, Pickett showed at Meadville, as he would later in his career, that he was a person who rose above the crowd to undertake tough challenges inspired by his unyielding sense of fairness.

Gene felt that the resident adults—in this instance, the faculty and administrative leaders—once again had failed him. Pickett was saying in effect: "You're not doing your job. I'm tired of the adults in my life defaulting on their responsibilities." So he finally resisted authority. He took a stand against a community of accountable adult governors whom he felt were not guiding the students toward mature, fulfilling work. The ministerial training that Meadville students were receiving was not complete. Gene was contending that ministry included more than academics, and Meadville's responsibility was to give and support its students in getting more.

This was a period of enormous growth for Pickett in self-confidence and inner strength. He could have deferred to Robbins and remained the safe, likable guy Robbins wished him to be. Instead of being the agreeable, obedient boy he had been during his formative years, Gene came of age as an adult who was willing to confront the religious establishment of his time and place.

One of the best antidotes to depression is healthy activism. The rebellion was a tough yet energizing process that reinforced Gene's therapy. He made personal strides even as he embodied a prophetic witness, and the insurgence changed the face not only of Meadville but also of Pickett himself. His being was deepened and his ministry readied by this controversial action. For Pickett, self-revelation and social reformation were joined in this period of creative turmoil at Meadville.

From Courtship to Marriage

> "No, not more light, but more warmth. We die of cold and not of darkness. It is the frost that kills and not the night."
>
> MIGUEL DE UNAMUNO

The Courtship

In 1952 Pickett resolved that he was going to graduate, complete therapy, and get married, all by the end of the school year. He had no prospects for a wife yet, but at least he had developed a plan. There were plenty of weekend parties at Meadville, and Gene had dated a number of women from the area without any serious romance developing.

Pickett actually had met Helen Rice the year before, introduced by a Chicago Theological Seminary/Meadville couple, Dorothy and Herb Vetter. Dorothy thought that more CTS women should meet more Meadville men, so she invited two women from CTS and two Meadville students to dinner at the Vetters' apartment. Helen Rice was one of them. She and Gene grew acquainted, but nothing came of the meeting. In fact, after their initial encounter, Helen was escorted home by the other man.

Despite administration objections, Pickett decided to seek a field work placement. One afternoon he simply walked across the street to the First Unitarian Church of Chicago and sought an assignment in the area of religious education. Helen had decided to do her field work under the tutelage of Edna Acheson, the splendid Religious Education Director at First Church as well. Gene and Helen were assigned to be co-leaders of the junior high group on Sunday afternoons. Helen was dating other people at the time, but clearly a romantic interest started brewing between the two seminarians. Gene perceived Helen to be the "All American Girl"—healthy, ebullient, pleasant—radically different from his earliest sweetheart, Gladys, less needy than his mother, and possessed of a personality in stark contrast to his own. Helen was spontaneous and playful and could, with some effort, elicit those same qualities in Gene.

The youth group was filled with the bright, eccentric, and immature offspring of University of Chicago faculty members like Enrico Fermi. No matter how interesting the planned program for a meeting might be, one or another member of the youth group could derail the intended purpose with off-the-wall comments and behavior. Helen was intimidated by these unpredictable displays, but Gene kept rising to the challenge of salvaging a constructive group experience out of the impending wreckage.

The incident Helen remembers most clearly was the day one of the young people brought in a copy of *Lady Chatterley's Lover*. This book was then unobtainable in the United States, but the junior higher had come upon a copy his mother had brought back from Europe. Immediately, there was much reading and giggling in a corner of the room. Gene suggested that the teenagers share the book openly with the entire group and encouraged them to read some of it aloud. Fortunately, Gene had studied some D. H. Lawrence in a literature course, had read *Lady Chatterley's Lover*, and could talk intelligently about Lawrence's views on love. A half-way profitable discussion ensued. Helen still wonders how Gene had captured a copy of the banned book himself!

Helen was a naive, innocent young woman from a small town in Oregon and was duly impressed that Gene could deal so constructively with these obstreperous kids. She admired his leadership and resiliency and found him definitely intriguing. In the effort to cope successfully with this recalcitrant junior high group, Helen and Gene had more and more frequent planning sessions. The group fell apart before the end of the year, but Gene and Helen were developing a thinly disguised courtship.

Helen had dated a number of men, but as a whole person, Gene was more engaging. Helen was a minister's daughter, and her father was a caring but heavy-handed and austere man. Like Gene, she had gone to seminary for her own self-discovery, not so much for a career, although she was interested in "doing good" through social, settlement house, or missionary work.

Helen was born in South Africa, the third of four children of Congregational missionaries to the Zulus. Her brother Lincoln was the oldest child, and Helen was sandwiched in age between the older sister Cynthia and her younger sister Julia. Her parents, Norman and Eunice Rice, shared an enlightened attitude toward mission work. They were not so much interested in "converting the heathen" as in working with people to improve their health, education, and living conditions. Her parents took immense pride in helping to develop black leadership in the mission schools, which later closed under apartheid. Those were important years to Helen and her family. She remembers the geography, the sound of hymns as they were sung in the African churches, and the time she was bitten by a monkey!

The Great Depression cut short their work in South Africa, and it was a disappointment to the Rice family to return to the United States where Helen's father served a series of small town and country churches in Oklahoma, South and North Dakota, and Oregon. These Home Mission churches were subsidized by the denomination so that they could afford even a part-time minister. The minister and his family received "missionary barrels" of clothing and linens from wealthier metropolitan churches.

During these years, Helen's father regularly preached three worship services a Sunday in three different churches, and the family invariably trundled along, attending all church services and Sunday school sessions. It was a physical ordeal, driving more than 100 miles every Sunday over gravel roads and returning home after midnight with sick headaches all around.

Helen did appreciate numerous aspects of being part of a minister's family. She always enjoyed the people, the attention lavished upon the children, and new experiences such as visiting the farms of rural church members. The truth was, as Helen phrased it, "In looking back, it appears that I was programmed from birth to become a minister's wife."

She recollects, "With hindsight, I can see now that my subconscious was vigorously at work on the idea of my marrying a minister. It was twenty more years before I realized that not my father but my mother was the key figure in my life—bright, educated, practical, no-nonsense, accepting, flexible—and I admired her very much. I saw her as leading a worthwhile and interesting life as the wife of a minister. Incidentally, my two sisters also married ministers!"

The welfare of the Rice children was important to their parents, who strove to provide them with broad experiences and travel despite severely limited financial resources. Education was a top priority for the three daughters as well as for the son, and they knew they would go to college. The Rices always had a piano in the house, and later, other musical instruments, too. All four children took piano lessons for years, whether they wanted to or not. Though Helen resented the mandatory aspects of taking piano lessons, she grew to love music and it provided her with most of her social contacts in church and school as the family migrated from town to town. Music remains a joyful, integral part of her life.

The Rices felt like outsiders in these small communities, especially because Helen's parents were often the most highly educated people in the town. Her parents' religious point of view could be described as Unitarian Christian and heavily influenced by the Social Gospel. Despite his liberal religious stance, Helen's father had a somewhat rigid, authoritarian personality. Helen was a child with a lot of spunk, to which he reacted in a fairly inflexible manner, so the combination of their personalities caused father and daughter no end of trouble. As Helen's mother confided years later, he was a good man but hard to live with.

Helen attended three different high schools and graduated in Milton-Freewater, Oregon. She qualified to be valedictorian of her class, but was denied this honor by a rule requiring her to attend that school for two years instead of the one year she had attended. Choosing a college illustrated how her life was directed by her parents, especially by her father. She took cues from her older sister who had argued hard for attending the University of Oregon to no avail. Her parents had decided on Whitman College in Walla Walla, Washington, for Cynthia, so when Helen's turn arrived, she knew there was no point in debating the issue and she willingly entered Whitman. Whitman was an excellent liberal arts college, similar to Oberlin. Nonetheless, Helen had had no voice in the decision.

Helen worked her way through college with summer jobs in canneries and fruit-packing houses and with campus jobs that paid her room and board. Helen loved college life, largely because it was her first opportunity to have some independence and to make her own decisions. Although she lived in a dormitory only twelve miles from home, it seemed farther because in those days most people, including the Rice family, did not make long distance phone calls unless it was an emergency. When you wanted to communicate with home, you wrote letters or sent postcards.

Helen started college in the fall one year after the end of World War II. The veterans were returning, and there were plenty of men on campus. The social life was organized around the Greek fraternity and sorority system. The Rice girls were not allowed to join sororities, both because they were expensive and because they were exclusive, the latter a point of principle with which Helen came to agree. However, this decision meant that once again Helen was something of an outsider, although she became president of the Independent Women's Organization and earned her share of campus honors for scholarship and leadership. Helen majored in Biology and was absorbed in musical activities.

When it came time to graduate from Whitman, Helen was perplexed about what she might do next. Generally for women of that era, the next important objective was matrimony, but Helen knew she wasn't ready for marriage because she had not yet figured out her view of life. Once again, Helen took the lead from her older sister, who had graduated two years ahead of Helen and entered the theological school at the University of Chicago, the school their father had attended. In listening to Cynthia and their father talk about her sister's plans, Helen was attracted to the idea that theological school offered an opportunity to clarify the meaning of your life within a community that encouraged you to think for yourself.

That opportunity was just what Helen yearned for, so she entered the Chicago Theological Seminary, then Congregationalist, now United Church of Christ. She had no definite career goals in mind, although she harbored an interest in becoming a missionary. She had no intention of marrying a minister, because her father had been a difficult spouse, yet Helen was too naive to know that women who attended seminary at that time were believed to be in search of a marriageable male minister. Helen does recall that President Dr. Cushman McGiffert, upon interviewing the entering women students, would ask them whether they were there to get an M.A. or a Mrs.

Helen loved school life and thrived on being exposed to new and expansive ideas. She entered the Bachelor of Divinity degree program, the professional degree for the ministry, but she chose to take the courses rather than to prepare for a specific career. Chicago Theological Seminary furnished two intense and significant years for her psycho-spiritual development. Helen explored seriously the neo-orthodox theological position that then commanded much interest and attention at Chicago, but she soon returned to the liberal religious position with which she had arrived.

Helen was not sure whether she would ever work in the church, but she knew she wanted to make her life count for something. She also needed to explore what she believed about significant emotional and spiritual issues before she chose the person she was going to marry. Her path was the reverse of that expected for women by people such as psychoanalyst Erik Erikson, who contended, "Women delay identity formation until they see whom they are going to marry."

Helen dated a number of the men at seminary and found many of them wanting. Gene was fascinating and even more desirable because he was uncertain about becoming a minister. He was a complex person who both attracted and perplexed the impressionable Helen.

She found Gene enigmatic, but sensed that he was interested in her. Because Gene was reticent to declare his intentions, she never quite knew where he stood with respect to their relationship. He took her to nice places, having learned something of the good life from Gladys. Helen, who had been raised poor, kept wondering where he got his spending money. She learned that Gene was working several jobs to pay off his debts and achieve some financial independence. Because her father had made a virtue of self-denial, Helen saw the ministry as an economically deprived way of life, which she wanted to avoid. Yet here was this man, also a product of the depression, who enjoyed nice things and lovely places.

Externally, Helen was a confident person, but internally she was insecure and unsure about whether she wanted Gene to pursue their relationship further. Because she was ambivalent about her feelings toward Gene, she didn't want to entice him to propose to her because down deep she wasn't sure she would answer, "Yes."

As their courtship grew more serious, Helen thought Gene had surely taken her for some "pheasant under glass" in order to use the occasion, in a setting suffused with romance and candlelight, to broach his intentions about their shared future. Just when she thought Gene was going to "pop the question," he blurted out, "Well, my friends are back at Meadville mimeographing some important documents, and I promised I'd get back to help them. Sorry, Helen, but we have to leave!" The student rebellion took precedence over their flourishing romance. Helen was crestfallen. "Okay," she mused, "I guess I'm just reading too much into our courtship."

The irony was that Gene did not think Helen was really drawn to him. "Why would she be interested in me?" was the underlying refrain of his impostor malaise. Helen was a popular person who in her love life had been tendered numerous marriage proposals. Most of them drew no serious interest from her, and although she considered herself good company, she, too, suffered from bouts of insecurity.

In reflecting back on their courtship, Gene notes, "I felt that I was all screwed up, and she was a good, hearty, All-American girl. I was fearful of being rejected, so for a long time, I decided I would rather be alone than risk rejection." After all, Gene had been alone most of his life and was familiar, if not comfortable, with that state. He had not received sufficient emotional sustenance from family members or anybody else, so this blossoming relationship with Helen presented a radical challenge to him. It would be frightening to graduate from a solitary world to one of potential intimacy.

A crucial episode occurred that deepened their bond. During her second year at CTS, Helen received an invitation from her brother Lincoln in Norfolk, Virginia, who was married and had a baby girl. Lincoln phoned and asked if she would come down and spend the Christmas holidays with them. Helen did not know her brother well because he had joined the Navy when she was twelve years old, so this was an attractive opportunity to spend some time with him and his family.

She mentioned it to Gene, and he said, "Why don't you go? I'm going to be in Washington. I can meet you at the airport and put you on the bus." He knew how to get to Norfolk, since he had been stationed there in the Navy. Helen knew little about traveling on her own and was anxious about making the arrangements. Gene helped her with everything.

There was a snowstorm, and Helen was one of the last students to leave the school because she had stayed behind to play the organ for a friend's wedding. When she arrived at the airport, it was mobbed, and all planes were grounded. Helen felt utterly alone there. Nobody knew that she was stranded in Chicago. She had only her plane ticket and wasn't sure what she would do if the plane didn't take off. She didn't even have enough money for taxi fare.

People sat on their suitcases anxiously passing the hours into the night. Everything was canceled. Finally, they called out her flight number, yet Helen was still apprehensive because this was her very first flight. She had no idea whether Gene would figure out what had happened to her. Nervous because the weather was still bad, she boarded the plane and took off. Meanwhile Gene was staying at Mary Crook's home in Washington, rising from time to time and phoning the airport to obtain precise information concerning Helen's arrival. When her plane landed, steady, trustworthy Gene was waiting for Helen. It was five o'clock in the morning. It had been an all-night ordeal for both of them. In their brief courtship, this was a memorable, defining moment when Gene had demonstrated his abounding concern and affection by taking care of Helen.

During his final whirlwind year at Meadville, Gene was completing therapy and preparing to graduate, but his relationship with Helen was still hanging. It was the March spring break, and Gene would soon be leaving Chicago to start his internship with Joe Barth in Miami. Things were getting tense. Gene took Helen out for one final dinner, and she thought he would say something definitive about their relationship, since he was leaving shortly and she would not see him again. But he failed to declare his intentions, and again Helen, uncertain herself, was not sure she wanted him to. But she did want the two of them to explore together the possibility of their shared future.

There was nothing predestined about their getting married, and it almost didn't happen. Helen decided fortuitously to stay in the dorm during spring break instead of visiting her Aunt Clara. She happened to attend an event at First Church, and Gene happened to be present as well. At the close of the program, Gene approached Helen and said, "Let's go to Jimmy's (the neighborhood tavern and student hangout) for a drink." Finally he asked Helen if she would consider marrying him. Would he have proposed to Helen even if they hadn't chanced upon one another that night?

Helen answered Gene with her own ambivalence: "Gene, I'm half in love with you." His approach had been circuitous; her response was equivocal. Yet both were finally ready to talk further about marriage. Gene invited her to come home to Maryland with him. Helen hesitated because she would be forced to miss the first week of the new term, and she was the sort of dutiful person for whom it was difficult to choose not to meet what she saw as an obligation. She also had no money. Gene said he would cash in a couple of government bonds to buy her ticket, and she could stay at his mother's house. Wanting to explore the possibility of marriage, she agreed to go to Maryland.

Helen stayed for several days, meeting all his family at the same time that she was deciding about Gene. This was the first and only time she would meet Gene's father, who was very ill and died shortly thereafter. Ollie was relatively uncommunicative, yet cordial to Helen. Cora, recognizing immediately that this woman was markedly different from Gladys, was warm and hospitable. Helen remembers being deeply touched by the gentle way Gene played with his nieces and nephews.

They talked interminably during the week, and at long last, one evening while seated on the sofa, Gene and Helen mutually agreed to get married. It was a shared proposal, and while Helen didn't feel madly in love with Gene, she was clear: "I would really like to take a chance on this guy!" Despite her doubts, she remained optimistic that this was what she wanted to do, and she never changed her mind. Gene felt greater certainty once he was able to verbalize his commitment.

Gene took the train to his Miami assignment, and Helen returned to school to complete the term. Gene returned to Chicago in June for his graduation and wedding. Helen did not finish her CTS career, putting Gene's aspirations before her own. She never had possessed a burning desire to complete her theological training. The degree itself meant little to her, and she did not feel shortchanged.

They were married on June 11, 1952 at the First Unitarian Church of Chicago by their respected minister and friend, Leslie Pennington. Family was important to Helen's parents, but they chose to miss the wedding because of the cost of travel, and only met Gene five months later. Helen

and Gene had chosen Chicago for the ceremony because
that was where their mutual friends lived. Gene's father was
terminally ill in bed, but Cora wouldn't miss her youngest
son's wedding for the world. She felt Helen was just the right
kind of person for Eugene. His cousin echoed the same sentiment when she said, "This was the best one you've ever
brought home, Eugene. Grab her!" Helen's sister, Cynthia,
was able to participate as the matron of honor because she
and her husband were visiting the Midwest on a trip from
California.

Helen posted invitations on the Meadville and CTS bulletin boards—"Helen Rice and Gene Pickett invite all their

Helen and Gene on their wedding day, June 11, 1952.

friends to share in their wedding." Seventy-five people attended what was considered, by one and all, a lovely celebration. Carl Wennerstrom was the best man, Clarke Wells and Emil Gudmundson were ushers, and Bob Kiefer sang a solo in his beautiful tenor voice. Helen walked down the aisle by herself.

Making Peace With Father

On their wedding day, Gene and Helen flew to Miami where Gene would resume his internship. Less than one month later Ollie Pickett died of emphysema at the age of sixty-three.

In the later years, Gene and his father had grown clumsily closer. Gene developed a progressive appreciation for the struggles that his father had endured. He was also impressed and proud that his father had been able to give up drinking without outside help. Toward the end of his life, Ollie bought Gene an old second-hand car, characteristically making his emotional connections through material objects rather than verbal communication. They were never able to share their lives and feelings with each other in their conversations.

Ollie was a quiet and gentle man, qualities that Gene recalls. Most people in the town remembered Ollie fondly as a likable guy who was responsive to people in need. That responsiveness galled Cora, because Ollie would frequently help people without getting paid for it. Gene replayed his father's behavioral scenario during his years of ministry, invariably giving more time to other people than he gave at home, behavior that caused grievous marital anguish. At one point, when Helen complained that Gene wasn't home more, he poignantly replied that he never knew what a father was supposed to do. As a steady breadwinner he would succeed where his father had failed, but he perpetuated the cycle of absence and alienation, because he still didn't know how to be present for his wife and children.

Gene had never heard his father voice pride in his sons or even speak of his love for them out loud, but at the end of Ollie's life, Gene felt that they had made some peace, perhaps sufficient peace.

Ollie's death was both a loss and a relief to Gene's mother. There had been so much frustration and torment that Ollie's final departure from the family was something of a blessing. He was laid out in the bedroom where Eugene had been born. An old-fashioned country viewing, funeral, and elaborate meal ensued. There was no public weeping, for the Picketts were a stoic family of a formal era.

Weathering a Crisis

During their time in Miami a severe car accident disabled Helen. It happened a scant five months after they were married. They had been vacationing with friends in Chicago and were navigating the almost three-day trip back to Miami. When they reached central Florida, they had a dreadful auto accident. Gene dolefully recalls that they had been arguing in the car and that Helen was driving without a license.

They were about three hours outside of Miami. It was two o'clock in the afternoon with perfectly clear, cool November weather. Helen was driving on a two-lane highway. She pulled up behind a big, eighteen-wheel truck as they were navigating a long curve. She looked around the bend to the right of the truck ahead and thought there was no traffic. They were driving a small car, their new English Hillman. Helen revved up the engine in order to pass, and, much to her shock, confronted two cars coming toward her. She swerved back behind the truck, and missed hitting either of the cars, but the Hillman spun totally out of control. People who saw the accident from a porch up the road said the car turned over three times. Helen was thrown out, Gene was not.

Helen was deeply stunned but not unconscious. She lay in a ditch far out in the countryside. She sustained a severe concussion that lasted for weeks, blurring her consciousness. No one remembers who got help, but it came quickly. Gene felt helpless because he couldn't find his glasses. Without them the world was a blur. He sustained only a bruised foot, yet he could not find Helen.

When he found her, she said, "Don't move me, it's my back." Helen couldn't move her legs without excruciating pain. When the ambulance came, they had to tilt her on her back and carefully straighten her out. She was rushed to a Seventh Day Adventist county hospital that was renowned for its expert medical care. If she had gone to any other hospital in the area, she might not have survived.

They X-rayed her and found she had two badly crushed vertebrae. Gene dissolved in tears when he told Helen that night of her condition. She was suffering so much from shock that the doctors did not believe she would make it through the night. Gene called Helen's parents, whom he had never met, to convey the news that their daughter was not expected to live. Her spine had been knocked out of line by half an inch. The only reason the cord had not snapped was that those two vertebrae were so broken apart that the spinal cord weaved through. The orthopedist who attended Helen said that he had never seen anyone survive injuries as serious as hers. If Helen did live, the medical team were not sure she would ever walk again. In any case, the family knew it was going to be a very long and strenuous road to recovery.

Gene was twenty-seven and Helen was twenty-three. They had only been married a matter of months. Helen stayed in that hospital until mid-January. She was in terrible pain, both physically and psychologically, and although the Picketts had little money, they hired a special-duty nurse to bolster her flagging morale.

The medical staff needed to stabilize her back but didn't dare touch the crushed vertebrae for fear they would slice the spinal cord. They ascertained immediately that there was some nerve damage to her left leg. The doctors decided to keep her still and under traction. It was two months before her bones had knit enough to undergo further treatment.

Carl Wennerstrom, who had been a dear, supportive friend and an important role model for Gene during the Meadville days, came down to be with him for about a week. The church people in Miami responded generously. Helen needed thirty pints of blood over those first weeks, and parishioners contributed unstintingly. A member of the church had a private plane, so he would regularly fly Joseph Barth and the fresh blood supply to the hospital. The Miami Unitarian church gave Gene a two-month, paid leave of absence to stay with Helen, and the hospital provided him with a room on the top floor so he could be nearby.

Visitors were not aware that Helen's concussion affected her vision, causing her to become dizzy and nauseated whenever anyone approached closely. When Barth, for example, came close to offer support and hold her hand, she would often vomit uncontrollably. The more he acted like her caring father, the sicker she would become. When the hospital chaplain visited her, she would get nauseous as well. In addition, the chaplain's theology offended Helen, because he proposed that God had clearly saved her from death for some higher purpose. She requested that the chaplain stop visiting.

Gene was profoundly frightened by not knowing what was going to happen to Helen. Neither of them knew throughout the entire hospital stay how things would turn out, but he remained emotionally stable and did not sink into depression. Helen was ignorant about either hospitals or medical personnel, but Gene, due to his extensive work as a medical corpsman in the Navy, knew the ins-and-outs of nursing. "He was remarkable," recalls Helen. "I can't imagine another young groom who would have known how to be so genuinely helpful in looking after my comfort. His patience was incredible. This was the opening of a whole other side of Gene I had not a clue about. He knew how to deal with doctors and nurses, what to ask, and how to see that we got the attention we needed. Otherwise, I was utterly helpless."

The hospital built a special bed for Helen so she would not have to be moved, and she remained under forty pounds of traction for two months. It was finally decided that Helen was sufficiently stabilized to be moved to Miami. They made a special brace for her and, without her ever sitting up, they drove her in an ambulance directly to a hospital in Miami. A doctor in the Unitarian Church had procured an orthopedist who consented to take her on as a patient at no cost. This generous man donated thousands of dollars of work for Helen's welfare. Gene was earning $133 a month, and they had no insurance. Given the financial resources the Picketts possessed, the costs were still high in spite of the doctor's generosity.

Helen was released to return home and convalesce there in a hospital bed designed for her. Gene guided Helen through her rigorous physical therapy for a month to strengthen her legs. Then they brought her back to the hospital for surgery to fuse the lower part of her spine. She stayed in the hospital for two weeks, then recuperated at home in a body cast for three more months, still not knowing whether the fusion would be successful or whether she would walk again. Somebody had to be with Helen at all times.

Gene and Helen spent their first Thanksgiving, Christmas, and New Year's Day together in the hospital. Helen's parents came after Christmas and stayed with members of the church. They would spend every day with Helen when Gene went off to work. Strangely enough, it seemed her parents were more upset to discover that Helen smoked cigarettes than they were about the condition of her back. Gene's mother came and helped as well. Although they were surrounded by loving family until May, it was an arduous and anguished winter for this newly married couple serving their first parish.

Gene was ordained at the First Unitarian Church of Miami on February 28, 1953; and Helen, after her spinal fusion surgery in January, was brought to the ordination lying on a stretcher in a house coat, replete with slippers and an orchid. It was a dramatic, celebratory moment for both Helen and Gene. Joseph Barth's wife, Ramona, sized up her duty as Helen's older compatriot in Miami and inquired whether there was anything she would like to do during her convalescence. Helen wanted to make an afghan, so Ramona Barth had church friends contribute money and materials for an afghan that Helen knitted for months, until it was finished. Ramona also commandeered a station wagon with the back seats removed to take Helen, on her stretcher, on enjoyable outings to visit people and places. Joseph and Ramona Barth were responsive, dutiful, and loving companions during this horrendous ordeal.

When Helen was somewhat up and about, she set about trying to be useful to Gene in his two-year ministry in Miami. He sought out and relied on her judgment and advice. He asked her to critique his sermons before he delivered them. For a period of time she was church organist, and she also organized a vacation church school. Essentially, however, the Picketts' time in Miami was focused jointly on Helen's recuperating from her automobile accident and Gene's establishing his call to the parish ministry. Helen was not fully ambulatory until approximately the time they decided to move on.

This traumatic episode strengthened their marriage, and both felt that, after weathering this crisis together, there would never be another difficulty in their lives too great for them to endure.

Miami: Trial by Fire

"You must do the thing you think you cannot do."

ELEANOR ROOSEVELT

Going South

When the Picketts first went South in 1952, Gene was still confused and unsure about ministry as a career. He left Miami quite definite that being a religious professional was his lifelong summons.

It was an exciting time of renewal for the Unitarian movement in 1952. New fellowships were being formed across the continent, and there was a mood of expansion and enthusiasm. The Southern climate had never been very hospitable to liberal religion. Only four Southern Unitarian churches had survived the Civil War, and that number had grown to only nine by the late 1940s. When Gene arrived in Miami, there were only eleven Unitarian churches and nine ministers in the eight states from Virginia to Florida and from the Mississippi to the Atlantic. Within the previous five years, twenty-one fellowships had been formed, but congregations were still few and far between.

As Gene remembers, "Being a Unitarian minister or layperson was a lonely affair, but spirits were high, the potential for growth was great, and the feeling of being part of a larger movement sustained and buoyed us. This feeling of being connected (and we would travel hundreds of miles to maintain those connections) was exceedingly important. This was before interstate highways, and it took two days just to get out of Florida. Indeed, if there had not been this sense of being part of a larger Unitarian community, many of those small groups would never have survived."

Joseph Barth

Gene's senior colleague in Miami, Joseph Barth, would vacate the church each year from May to October in order to rest from chronic heart problems, and a student minister would fill in for him for almost half the year. When Gene told Barth that he had never been a minister, and that the church could conceivably crumble with him there alone, Barth retorted, "Well, if the church falls apart it will just demonstrate that I haven't done a very good job of building it, so whatever you want to do, you do." Gene was so successful as an intern minister that the congregation called him as their first full-time assistant minister. The Picketts stayed for two years.

Barth had two months to prepare Gene for the internship before he left for Maine. He proved to be a good mentor and played a fatherly role as well, a bond that lasted until his death in 1988. Barth was deeply invested in the persona of the mentor-father, and since that was exactly what Gene desired, too, the tie between them was a happy congruence of needs. As the years passed, Barth never fully dropped the father-son attachment with Gene and would continue to encourage and praise him in a parental fashion, with words like "I could have told you so," even when Gene became president of the Unitarian Universalist Association.

Yet the formative ministerial influence of Joseph Barth on Gene Pickett cannot be underestimated. In 1985, thirty-three years after Gene first went to Miami, he had an opportunity to honor Barth publicly with these words: "When I went to Miami to serve as student minister with Joe Barth, I was unfamiliar with Unitarian churches and naive about ministry. I was uncertain and insecure, in other words, scared to death. If my first experience in the parish had not been with Joe Barth or his clone, I doubt if I would have remained in the ministry. . . . Joe was mentor and counselor, father and big brother, colleague and friend—all wrapped up together."

Barth had a reputation throughout the city of Miami as a fine counselor and would pack his day with hourly appointments. When Joe left for Maine, Gene maintained some of Barth's considerable counseling load. Pickett's immersion in his own therapy gave him the tools to assist others during their personal trials and tribulations. During Barth's absence, Gene assumed organizational responsibilities in a church known for its loosely structured operation, and Gene's gifts as an administrator were soon evident.

Barth was the first man who spent time with Gene and said, "You can do it, you can be a minister!" When Gene would demur or confess that he was uncertain, Barth would press, "Well, what would you rather do?" And Gene would reply, "Maybe I could write children's books!" Until the day he died, Barth would playfully remark, "Well, Gene, have you decided yet whether you're going to write children's books or stay in the ministry?"

Learning the Ropes

The Miami church building was only half-constructed, so the setting was casual, if not unkempt. The sanctuary roof was missing, so services were held in the social hall. Church attendees lounged around in dining room chairs and sofas—and even smoked—during informal worship services. In this all-purpose room, other parishioners would sit way back in the kitchen drinking coffee, and listening over the loud-speaker. Sounds of the road spilled into the service center from the nearby Dixie Highway, trains went by on the other side, and planes buzzed overhead. And, there was no air conditioning! Needless to say, this was a most difficult setting for a neophyte minister to sustain inspirational liturgy. Later, when the highway was expanded, the building was demolished and the church received enough compensation to rebuild in a better location.

Always aspiring to look appropriately groomed, a habit carried over from childhood, Gene would arrive for church services well-attired with tie and coat. Such garb proved far too formal for the Floridian milieu, yet Gene never grew accustomed to preaching with an open sport shirt. Joe Barth donned a "uniform"—a white linen suit that served as his trademark. During the week, Pickett would wear a suit to the office even when the weather was brutally hot. He would go home at lunch time to change his sweat-drenched shirt.

The Miami church was an unusual combination of two constituencies: the Sunday morning congregation and the Wednesday night forum attended by many from the political left. The two groups only partially overlapped. Gene was placed in charge of the forum, and his responsibilities included securing the speakers and moderating the programs. The forum was an established tradition that attracted distinguished winter visitors to Miami to serve as presenters. Fritz Perls, Helen and Scott Nearing, and Mary McLeod Bethune were representative of the regulars who attracted large audiences.

This was an era when Communists were being blacklisted in the United States. There were a number of people in the Miami congregation who had been, or were reputed to have been, Communists, and the story of their presence in the church blew up in the newspaper that summer of 1954. Joe made a special trip from Maine to preach a sermon on the inclusive church where everybody was welcome. The next day's headline read: "Homosexuals and Reds Welcome At First Unitarian Church." The church received both flak and commendation.

Gene was also learning the ropes with respect to pastoral calls. He reports his first visit in a letter written to Helen, six days after arriving on the job in Miami: "Dearest Helen, I am about to make my first parish call, or rather it is the other way around. I am waiting for the chauffeur to call for me and take me to some hotel bathing club. I am to meet the granddaughter of a woman who supposedly owns half the sugar plantations in Puerto Rico. What this is doing for my delusions of grandeur you can well imagine!

"This type of thing is always an anxiety-creating situation for me. I suspect I am still not sure of myself. There is always the feeling, "What shall I do?" or "How shall I dress?"—the fear of making a blunder. There is also the mixed feeling of wanting to be a part of this type of life while at the same time being contemptuous of it. I have to keep saying to myself, "Be yourself!" This is one of the problems I have been working on, and my reaction to this situation indicates that I still have to keep at it. My problem being: thinking and pretending that I am something other than what I am!

"The next day: When I left off yesterday, my parish call arrived with chauffeur and all. Susie is a 19-year-old Puerto Rican art student in New York who is spending her spring vacation with her grandmother, a friend of the church. Also in the party was her grandmother, who speaks only Spanish, and her translator.

"We went to a cabana club at a downtown hotel that included a beautiful swimming pool, cocktail terrace, and dining room. Susie and I were left there for a swim, drinks, and lunch. We had a good talk about Unitarianism, religion, and art, and some of her family problems, which she has plenty of. Susie was intelligent, sensitive, and really interested in religion. At the appointed time we heard, 'The car is waiting,' and I was once again a scrubby old ministerial intern!"

Gene and Helen were well liked in Miami. A lot of his success there and in later ministries was due to the fact that he paid considerable and constant attention to people. He was personable and cared genuinely and directly about people. Gene was a keen reader of human nature. He perceived what people wanted, in spite of what they might have said, and he assisted them in obtaining or accomplishing what it was they sought. In *Taoism of Leadership,* a passage describes Pickett's gift as a minister: "Gentle interventions, if they are clear, overcome rigid resistances. If gentleness fails, try yielding or stepping back altogether. When the leader yields, resistances relax. . . . Few leaders realize how much how little will do."

Pickett describes his own pastoral manner in this way: "My style has been a quiet attentiveness to the thoughts and feelings of others. I have always worked to help people realize their own goals. I have striven to reconcile differing views so that each feels heard and included. I have consistently emphasized the necessity of building a strong institution if the values and ideals of our liberal faith are to be influential in the larger society. I have tried to share not only my ideas and ideals but also my humanness."

First Sermon

In his entire seminary career Gene had only delivered one sermon, so he arrived in the Miami pulpit as a greenhorn. Barth did not help him directly with sermon construction or content, but Gene did follow Barth's pattern of carting small half-sheets of text into the pulpit. Along the way Gene also received the critical yet sage advice: "In time, Reverend, you'll get so you preach only one sermon at a time!" Most of Pickett's homilies were topical, essentially mini-lectures with minimal self-disclosure, a mode that satisfied the predominantly intellectual Miami congregation. There was, however, one touchstone sermon that Gene preached in Miami, and worked variations upon during his entire career. It was entitled "Salvation in Our Time," an address focusing on his quest to discover his own salvation via the profession of ministry.

Beginning in Miami, Pickett grasped the important lesson of balancing his sermon topics among the historical, theological, political, and psychological dimensions of human reality. In the early years of his career, Pickett's sermons were well researched and heavily rational. Only later would his addresses become more revealing of the inner life. His manner of preaching was never contrived or ornate, yet in his unaffected, natural way, he touched the soul of his listeners by explicating his own humanity. People could identify with him. Through his own struggles, he conveyed a helpful and healing message.

Pickett has always acknowledged the pastoral role as the primary strength of his parish work; his gift as a caring, responsive person would inevitably emerge through his sermons. He never indulged the impulse to use the pulpit as his own confessional or therapist couch. He retained personal privacy, but his unadorned humanity kept breaking through as he struggled openly with the thorny social and ethical quandaries of his life and time.

Pickett entered the ministry despite his anxieties about both preaching and writing. He chose to be a minister because it offered a genuine yet undefined way to "do good," not because he wanted to be an orator. Whenever he was called upon to speak publicly, be it a planned speech or an informal prayer, he was frightened. Despite his fear, he was able to reach people because of his inescapable authenticity. When Gene preached, his listeners felt "we are all in this together—he's agonizing with what we are all agonizing with."

An Evolving Humanism

The congregation was unapologetically humanist, and Gene was an unrepentant rationalist, so his theological disposition and his sermons on the current discoveries of psychology coincided with parishioners' interests.

Standing up, especially in the South, and railing against the views of fundamentalism would gain certain applause. However, Pickett never preached a consistently dogmatic humanism as was the practice of numerous Unitarian colleagues during this period. Being abrasive or exclusionary in word or deed was not consonant with his bedrock nature. Pickett's preaching manner was geared to make parishioners feel at home in the pluralistic, inclusive Unitarian Universalist heritage, no matter where their personal views might reside on the theological continuum.

Perhaps the primary lesson Barth transmitted to Gene was the importance of the Free Mind principle which, in turn, helped to fortify Gene's own embryonic Unitarian faith. This principle underlies the Unitarian Universalist liberty to believe anything that reason and conscience prompt us to believe as long as we grant others the same right. Pickett gained respect for Barth, the Miami congregation, and Unitarianism in general when he saw exemplars of goodwill negotiating their disagreements and conflicts in creative resolution.

People would sometimes rise in the Miami congregation and shout to someone across the room, "How can you be a Unitarian and say something like that!" Gene learned to intervene when necessary and say, "Remember, everyone belongs here who is willing to practice the principle of the free mind." Gene grew accomplished at keeping congregations from polarization by holding them to such governing principles as the "free mind."

Pickett became a religious leader who welcomed the strange opinion, the different position, the underdog. He was effective in large measure because he encouraged, even rewarded, dissent among his parishioners and staff members. He was hospitable to contrary convictions and differing perceptions—an essential quality in a truly enabling leader.

Pickett's beliefs and values were tied more closely to psychological insights than theological ones, drawing from existentialists such as Albert Camus and Victor Frankl, and psychologists such as Rollo May and Erich Fromm. During the course of Pickett's parish ministries, his entrenched humanism would mellow and evolve into a mystical naturalism. He grew to proclaim that there is a profound sense of connectedness discoverable in the human and natural realm, a relatedness that cannot be fully fathomed and remains forever inspirational.

In the early days of his ministry, Pickett would never use the term God, but as time progressed he would define God as a symbol for the highest values that we know, or, even more importantly, as a sense of kinship to one another and the greater universe. This resolute sense of interrelatedness remains the foundation of his theology.

As he grew into the job and developed his own style of ministry, the Miami congregation grew respectful and supportive of Gene, who looked as young as a teenager, a fact that customarily worked in his favor. They "adopted" him as their ministerial offspring, teaching him the ropes of church procedure and life. He became both son and minister-in-training. Miami was overall a good experience, and the Picketts still have friends from those days.

Lured to Richmond

"To sound a certain trumpet does not mean just trumpeting one's own certitudes. It means sounding a specific call to specific people capable of response."

GARY WILLS

A Traditional Liberal Church

During Gene's second year in Miami, he was the Sunday morning preacher at the Blue Ridge, North Carolina, Unitarian Summer Institute. Members of the First Unitarian Church in Richmond, Virginia, heard his address and were very impressed. The church was looking for a minister, and they contacted Pickett to ask him if he would be interested. The Picketts were not really ready to leave Miami, but their financial situation was borderline. The invitation was attractive because Richmond was offering a $7,000 salary in contrast to Gene's $4,000 income in Miami.

Furthermore, Pickett felt he would be fortunate to follow Dilworth Lupton in Richmond, and this helped them decide to accept Richmond's offer and leave Miami. Lupton had been a well-known Unitarian minister in Cleveland and had worked as a newspaper reporter earlier in his professional life. After Cleveland, he had served the congregation in Waltham, Massachusetts, then concluded his ministerial career with a three-year stint in Richmond. Lupton, a zealous advocate of advertising who specialized in provocative sermon titles, had done a skillful job of building up the Richmond congregation. He had also achieved considerable healing in the church amid the dissension fostered by the preceding ministry. Lupton had put the church back on the growing path and in good organizational shape before Pickett arrived.

The Picketts were now living in the old capitol of the Confederacy. The church was a solid, established, liberal congregation with strong, experienced lay leadership ready and willing to work with a new, young minister. The Picketts' experience there was a rich and satisfying one; during seven and one-half years in Richmond, Gene and Helen had three children, all daughters.

Lupton took a personal interest in Pickett's arrival, assuming a father-figure role similar to Barth's. He offered a variety of helpful administrative suggestions such as "one group you should pay constant attention to is the Finance Committee, but even more important is your regular input into the Nominating Committee process." Pickett still pictures Lupton down on the floor lighting the heater in the minister's study, showing him how best to manage this menial yet necessary task.

If Barth helped Gene with the psychological dynamics of the pastorate, Lupton focused on the organizational aspects of ministry. In contrast to Miami, the Richmond congregation was a solid, stable church that included a number of veteran Unitarians. As Gene remembers, "Several of these leaders had come from New England, and I attributed their commitment and loyalty to their New England background. That was before I moved to New England and discovered that commitment and loyalty are not necessarily characteristic of New England Unitarians!"

Yet Richmond was truly a teaching church, filled with committed institutionalists. Pickett is emphatic with his praise: "This church took a young, inexperienced, and naive recent graduate of theological school and helped make him into a relatively effective minister. If it had not been for the good experience we had in Richmond, I doubt that I would have survived in the ministry. It was there that I learned the basic skills of church organization and the dynamics of congregational life."

Race Relations

When Pickett had first arrived in Miami as a student minister, African Americans were not allowed on the streets of Miami Beach after sundown without work permits. Multiracial gatherings were illegal, and the Unitarian Church in Miami was one of only two places that would risk holding integrated meetings. Being a Unitarian was not only lonely, it was dangerous. Enormous changes in racial justice were to take place, but not without struggle and violence.

The Picketts moved to Richmond in 1954, the year of *Brown* v. *Board of Education of Topeka, Kansas,* the historic Supreme Court school desegregation decision. Some members of the congregation were ardent Republican conservatives, but they were staunchly liberal on the race-relations issue. Church membership included a number of African Americans, and the church maintained a high profile on integration issues.

Pickett's community activities were primarily in the area of race relations, serving as vice president of the Richmond Council on Human Relations, as chair of the Work Committee for the Friends' Association for Colored Children (an adoption and foster home care agency for African Americans), as a board member of the Virginia Council on Human Relations, and most industriously as chair of a state-wide Save Our Schools committee, fighting against the state's plan to change the constitution to permit the use of public funds for private schools.

Virginia was experiencing a major upheaval in race relations. It was the first state to threaten to close its public schools rather than integrate. It was also the state where the theory of interposition emerged. Interposition was the view that the United States was a voluntary federation of states, and that each state reserved the right to interpose itself between the federal government and state citizens. This doctrine was introduced in an attempt to block school desegregation.

Pickett was one of the few white ministers in the state to support the Save Our Schools effort. In a front-page newspaper clipping from the *Richmond Afro-American*, he is the only white person in the lineup of supporters listed in its annual Honor Roll. He regrets not possessing a keener sense of history at the time, yet it was not his nature to keep track of his personal involvements and prophetic accomplishments.

Pickett was uneasy with any prominent public role but felt impelled by conscience and duty to combat racial injustice. He stepped forward as a leader, often when no one else was willing to do so. He was driven by what he called a "terrible sense of oughtness." As he would confide to Helen, "The best I can offer is that people know they can count on me." Day in and day out, within the parish and beyond in the community, Pickett was indeed a rock of pastoral faithfulness and prophetic dependability.

His first protest march transpired in Farmville, Virginia, a central site of racial tension. For the first time, Pickett experienced the intransigent hate expressed by white people against blacks and their white sympathizers. He was spit on in this demonstration, and the situation grew gravely threatening because the police were supportive of the vengeful whites. Pickett remembers vividly this mean-spirited, ugly scene from which he has never morally recovered. He has generally considered himself a coward in public confrontations, but his participation in this dangerous protest would depict him as a courageous, even if hesitant, justice-builder.

Pickett would always be self-conscious in the public limelight. He did not possess the strong, if not overbearing, ego usually associated with prophets. He was embarrassed hobnobbing with famous people. There is a picture of Pickett's arrest in front of the South African Embassy in Washington, DC, during his tenure as UUA president. Gene is standing alongside other social activists making a commitment in support of the boycott against apartheid. In such public conflicts Pickett was uncomfortable being out front, whether speaking or marching. Yet he felt eternally summoned as a religious person and leader to "do good."

A UPI news feature captures Pickett's uneasiness as a public protester: "Eugene Pickett concedes that getting arrested, even when he won't have to spend any time in jail, makes him a little nervous. Pickett, president of the Unitarian Universalist Association and a longtime supporter of civil rights and anti-war causes, readily acknowledges that he had butterflies in his stomach, as the essentially private Pickett and thirty-six other Unitarian Universalists presented themselves for arrest in witness against apartheid at the South African Embassy in February of this year [1985].

"For Pickett it was his first act of civil disobedience, but the event also underscored the new public confidence of a religious liberalism that has recently been eclipsed by the resurgence of militant and political fundamentalism."

Gene's unbending commitment to racial justice first took root during his days in the military where he was deeply disturbed about the segregation present there. During his ministries in the South—Miami, Richmond, and later Atlanta—advocacy for racial harmony was his primary involvement in promoting social justice.

The Agony of Preaching

In Richmond, Gene's sermon writing was more disciplined than in Miami, but it was never an easy or smooth endeavor. Preaching remained a fierce struggle for Pickett for the duration of his career. He has been plagued by the dread disease called "sermonophobia," for Gene was consumed with the fear of rejection; the fear of exposing his secrets; the fear inherent in the Impostor Syndrome; just plain, raw fear. Yet fear can be a motivator as well as a paralyzer, so every week he experienced sufficient angst to produce a sermon. He attempted different strategies such as preparing the sermon by Tuesday or Thursday, but then he would just spend the entire week laboring on the sermon alone, deepening and lengthening his sense of anxiety. He finally settled on the Saturday plan, as aggravating as it was, and he and Helen would collaborate.

Gene would accomplish his reading and research during the week, but he wouldn't start writing or dictating until late Saturday night and would never go to bed until the early hours of Sunday morning. Saturday nights for either church or personal social life were off-limits for the Picketts. In Miami Gene did his sermon writing on his own, and Helen would do some editing. In Richmond a more grueling process began. Because of Saturday professional obligations, including retreats and rites-of-passage, Gene would not start composing until Saturday evening after supper was finished and the babies were in bed.

Helen recalls the whole ordeal as unmitigated torment, "like pulling teeth, preparing from scratch a major term paper every single Saturday night. I was plenty facile as a typist, but his words came agonizingly slowly. He wanted me to just sit there and wait. He did not want me to read books or anything. I had to stay alert and be ready to type whenever any words came forth. It was a terrible scene."

She would never write the sermon herself, but somewhere along the path, Helen would suggest, "Maybe you can say that better, Gene," and would help him rework his text even as she was typing. Her role was to catch any blatant problems and to cheer Gene on. This went on until 3, 4, or 5 o'clock Sunday morning, when they would go to sleep and arise scarcely a few hours later. They would get the children up and fed and leave about 9:00 A.M. for church. When they returned home about 1:00 P.M., they were both exhausted. They would put the babies in their cribs and collapse in a heap on their own bed. The whole merry-go-round was mounted again on Monday morning, when the next sermon title had to be conceived and named. Helen did this for three years, then rebelled saying, "I can't do this anymore. Somebody's got to be civil to our children." So she quit and Gene was back on his own.

Gene needed Helen's confirmation that his sermon was presentable, so he would read it to her before he delivered it. This provided a profitable warm-up as he psyched himself for the real delivery. Pickett would nervously query, "Is it all right? Is it all right?" and she would say "Yes, yes!" Gene has always remarked that Helen knew her line well.

Unlike many ministers who resist congregational response or input, Gene entertained the critique of parishioners. He treated them as his teachers, and he invariably had someone in the congregation who was self-delegated to criticize the substance and delivery of his sermons. In Richmond, there was Eudora Ramsey Richardson, writer and community activist, who, at the end of the Sunday morning service, would hand Gene a note listing the grammatical gaffes and mispronunciations he had produced in that sermon.

There was also Margaret Rackett, the epitome of the Southern gentlewoman and CEO of a sizable church envelope company, who had a passion for words and word games and helped Pickett markedly improve and increase his vocabulary. Then there were the Collisons, active in Richmond drama groups, who critiqued his sermon presentations as well. And Hazel Higdon cannot be forgotten. She, along with other volunteers, would sit every Sunday at a desk near the rear of the sanctuary taking attendance and preparing a list of absentees whom Gene should check on during the week. For a minister like Gene who welcomed such counsel and critique, he was surrounded by a bevy of helpful mentors.

Later in Atlanta, Gene would also benefit from an actress and speech therapist, Mary Nell Santacroce, who doubled as his drama coach. Early on, she audaciously told him that he was "doing terribly and needed some lessons." Never too haughty for help, indeed hungry for it, Pickett availed himself of whatever assistance this parishioner and other professionals could offer. Gene harbored a small ego and felt that if someone had constructive counsel to contribute, he would never be above taking it.

A Leader Matures

Gene sought guidance in areas other than preaching. He welcomed, often elicited, help from parishioners who were competent in various aspects of church life, like finances, an area where he gladly summoned the expert advice of business people in organizing fund drives. He never had to lead by himself. This collaborative style held him in good stead in his Southern ministries and later in the UUA presidency.

In Richmond Pickett expanded the overall program life by starting a choir, giving fuller structure to the worship service, and launching a resourceful adult education series. As a high-control and deeply enmeshed leader, Gene attended all committee meetings, a feat that would become the "backbreaker" in his Atlanta ministry.

Gene's presence did make a difference in people's lives. He was personal. He gave moral support and helped individuals succeed in their volunteer endeavors. He empowered laity. He didn't fit the conventional ministerial profile because he actually relished administrative work. His ministry came alive in the interpersonal exchanges of meetings and programs. He felt comfortable and highly confident in organizational work, less so as the performer on display in the pulpit or in other public roles.

Gene was adept at learning to manage and motivate people without manipulating them. He had an uncanny ability to read people, understand their aspirations, remember key alignments. His political abilities were exceptional. Gene always considered them instinctive. As he phrased it, "Once I was able to sense where people are, I would try to put them in positions of responsibility where they could be most effective. It was my conviction that the whole was greater than the sum of the parts, and that my ministerial job was to jell the different talents of a given congregation."

Gene was a leader, not a boss; the former engenders confidence in people, the latter creates fear. Pickett was always up front about enlisting people with whom he could work well, and he would forthrightly encourage nominating committees to select precisely those leaders. Because Gene elicited a high level of trust from people, he was an unthreatening broker and bridger. Gene was ubiquitous, invariably present to assist or guide, but he willingly allowed others to garner the acclaim.

In Warren Bennis's classic, *On Becoming a Leader,* he signals the four major ingredients leaders possess: constancy (leaders are all of a piece; they stay the course); congruity (leaders walk their talk; there is no gap between the theories they espouse and the life they practice); reliability (leaders are there when it counts; they are ready to support their co-workers in the momentous decisions); integrity (leaders honor their commitments and promises). Gene scored consistently high in all four areas.

The church in Richmond flourished, and soon there was insufficient space for the religious education program. Because they could not expand in their city location, the congregation bought a row house and converted it and the former parsonage into church school space. However, shortly after the Picketts moved on, the church decided to build on a new site. Gene was relieved that he did not have to mount a major capital fund drive during his tenure because he was not sure that it would have been successful.

In fact, Gene perennially felt ill-equipped to garner strong financial support from his own churches. Although he became an effective financial leader for the UUA during his presidency, he felt hamstrung in the local parish by the need to raise his own salary. He left Richmond basically because he thought they would never be able to pay a minister more than $9,000. Although he deserved more money, he refused to marshal the forces to justify his case. His successor asked that the salary be roughly doubled, and it was! But Gene believed he had accomplished in Richmond what he had set out to do: stabilize the congregation, expand the program life, and provide two new structures for religious education. There was no pressure for Gene to leave any of his parish ministries. He never abandoned a church nor was he forced out. He departed when conditions were solid.

From Richmond, Pickett explored possible posts from Santa Barbara to Syracuse. He also considered Baltimore, because "I wanted to go home and show everybody how a hometown boy can make good and all. But in candidating for Baltimore, I would reach a certain point, then blow it. I felt great anxiety and was hounded by the fear of rejection. The first time I tried for Baltimore, I simply withdrew in the process due to paralyzing ambivalence. The second time, eight years later, I self-destructed by doing something totally out of character, launching into a tirade about their financial management. The hometown boy shot himself in the foot!"

The Atlanta church became open, but the Picketts had reservations. They had three little children, and Helen recalls saying to Gene, "I just don't know whether it's a good idea to take these children and go even deeper South during such hostile times." Unitarian Universalist ministers were disinclined even to consider southern congregations during this era, knowing it was a reactionary area enmeshed in grave turmoil.

Because Helen's family had lived in ten locations during her youth, no specific region felt like home to her. If Helen were drawn to any place, it would be the Pacific Northwest. Gene was averse to leaving the East Coast because his mother lived there. Although the Picketts harbored doubts about continuing to live in the South, Atlanta was still familiar territory. They had close ministerial colleagues like Bob West and Bob Palmer in Tennessee, and Jim Brewer in Norfolk, Virginia, serving in the South alongside them. They knew there was work to be done in the South, and realized that Atlanta, a larger and more progressive city than Richmond, held substantial promise.

Making Peace With Mother

Therapy had enabled Pickett to disconnect from the smothering bond with his mother. Fortuitously, Cora was also freeing herself from her own dissatisfied life at about the same time.

A year or two after Gene's father died, Cora heard about a program in Washington, DC, that had been funded by Julius Garfinkel, the owner of Garfinkel's department store and a friend of All Souls Unitarian Church, also in Washington, DC. When Garfinkel died, he left the store to his employees and bequeathed an endowment to establish a school for women who, through divorce or death of a spouse, found they needed to earn a living. The Hannah Harrison School, named in memory of Garfinkel's mother, provided free training for all women who were accepted into the program.

Cora was sixty-two at the time, but she fudged her age to fit the application requirements. Once again, her survival instincts triumphed and she was accepted. After completing a nine-month food service program, Cora found a job at one of the hospitals in the Washington area. She moved into her own apartment, enjoyed managing her money, and was proudly launched upon the happiest period of her life.

With a lively curiosity about new places and experiences, Cora loved to travel and took a number of trips during these years. She was free of the anxiety and aggravation she experienced living on the financial brink during her marriage. She thrived on independence, and even confessed that, in truth, she had always hated Winfield. Cora lived resourcefully for twenty-five years in Washington, until she needed to live in a nursing home.

Gene and Helen lived in Richmond, Virginia, during this span of Cora's life, so they kept in close, caring touch with her. Cora would visit them as well, sometimes taking care of the three Pickett daughters. The girls were quite loving and responsive to Grandmother Cora, especially their oldest daughter Ann, now a nurse, who remarked when Cora was in the nursing home, "If anybody will know how to make the system work for her, it's grandmother!" They grew close, bantering spiritedly, even arguing, bypassing the intense parent-child struggles Gene and Cora had endured. Ann even became interested in working with older people because of the considerable time she spent with her Grandmother Cora. Clearly, being a grandmother was an easier and more gratifying role for Cora than being a mother.

In the early stages of their relationship, Cora irritated Helen with her narcissism. Cora personalized everything. She once told Gene and Helen how annoyed she was about the Vietnamese people who would persist in speaking their own language while riding on the same bus with her. Cora was sure they did it deliberately so that she wouldn't be able to understand them! Gene, armed with greater self-awareness and objectivity after therapy, would be the buffer between his mother and wife, moving to Helen's aid when necessary, and generally helping to sustain an atmosphere of peaceful co-existence.

Cora was ultimately proud that her son was a minister, although she would rarely express her esteem directly to Gene. When visiting in Richmond, she made friends with people in the congregation, and they would exchange admiring comments about Gene. By the time Gene became UUA president, Cora had joined the Universalist Church in Washington, DC. How this had come to pass was somewhat ironic. One day Cora was late for her regular Methodist church service, and so at 11 o'clock she dismounted the bus because she saw a church right there on a nearby corner. The congregation that happened to be located at the bus stop was National Memorial Universalist Church. The parishioners were friendly to her and invited her to attend their various activities that Sunday morning. The next week she returned, and soon thereafter joined this "nice, warm church," over time growing fond of its minister Dr. Seth Brooks.

Cora began to receive the Association publication *Unitarian Universalist World* and was justifiably pleased that her son was president of her newfound religious faith. She seldom said much about it, but Gene and Helen intuited her feelings. Strangely enough, Cora was the only member of the Pickett clan who ever developed any appreciation of Gene's successful professional life. Harry was gone. Gene's dad had died. And the other relatives never made the slightest effort even to hear him preach.

Cora reluctantly left Washington to enter a retirement home in Westminister, Maryland, near Marcus. She was not there long before she fell and broke her hip, an event that seemed to spell the beginning of the end. But Cora's conclusion was a long time in coming. She lived another six years in a nursing home, outliving her husband by three decades.

As UUA president, Gene wrote a regular column in the *Unitarian Universalist World* entitled "Pickett Lines." A portion of one column entitled "My Mother Is Waiting," read: "This fall my mother is waiting for death. Now, almost ninety-one years old, she recently suffered a stroke which paralyzed her left side. This followed the pain of a broken hip and a hip replacement over a year ago. And all the suffering is compounded by the crippling arthritis with which she has lived for many years. On our way to Smithton, Helen and I visited her. She is lying in a nursing home bed waiting. . . .

"So this fall I give thanks not only for the harvest of another year, but even more for a long life lovingly lived. And now, 'Come lovely and soothing Death . . . ,' my mother is waiting."

Stoical Gene sometimes wept during her lengthy, exhausting stay in the nursing home, and by the time Cora actually passed away, Gene had already said his emotional good-byes. If Gene had been asked to say something at his father's memorial service he would not have known what to offer at that point. But upon his mother's death he told other members of the family and the Methodist minister in the hometown Winfield church that he wanted to share some words.

Gene delivered a brief and honest tribute in summation

of her life: "At this final farewell to our mother and grandmother, I would like to add a few personal remarks. Mom was a strong, determined woman who overcame many difficulties in her long life. She lived with more illness than anyone else I know, and yet she lived to the age of ninety-six. She was a person of independent spirit, provident by nature, and ever protective of the family's well-being. She had the primary responsibility for raising us three boys during the depression—not an easy task.

"She was always keenly involved in our life and work, and this extended to her grandchildren as well. She took great personal pride in Marcus's accomplishments. She liked the sound of Judge Pickett. She lived through years of deep sorrow over Harry's death in World War II. It took many years for her to understand my becoming a Unitarian Universalist, but she was proud of my going into the ministry. She had a strong and lasting influence on our lives—positive and, sometimes, negative.

"The church was always an important part of her life. She was born and raised a Lutheran. When she married and moved to Winfield, she became a very involved Methodist. During her time in Washington she joined the Universalist church. She took comfort from the Universalist belief that in the end *all* souls will be united in harmony with God.

"The real sorrow of these past five or six years, for her and for us, came from her awareness that her independence, her body, and her spirit were wasting away. She had to wait too long for death to come. But we are thankful, for her sake, that it came at last, and we shall always be grateful for the memories that live on, for the love that was shared, and for the life that continues in us. As the poet wrote, 'Must death be proud to take a royal soul.'"

The service was held at the funeral home according to local custom. It was a beautiful, clear April day, marked by a crisp breeze. As the funeral procession drove along after the service, Helen and Gene could see Ebenezer Church and the graveyard across the fields. It was a lovely scene, and Gene was moved to remark, "Mom would have liked this!"

Moving On to Atlanta

A leader is best when people barely know he exists.
Of a good leader, who talks little,
When his work is done, his aim fulfilled,
They will say, "We did this ourselves."

FROM THE TAO TE CHING

Getting Started

Richmond was a congregation of 250 members; Atlanta had over 300. The Picketts moved to Atlanta in 1962 and were greeted by an exciting, boom-town atmosphere with considerable potential for growth. When they left twelve years later there were 1,150 members plus 200 who had left to form a new congregation. Gene preached to an average of over 850 people each Sunday, with 800 children in the church school program and nearly 2,000 participants in the adult education program.

Pickett was chosen from a list of candidates that included Bob West. These two friends would later jest and jab about this quirk of fate, since both would become UUA presidents. Bob West went from Knoxville, Tennessee, to Rochester, New York, shortly after the Picketts moved to Atlanta.

Pickett's predecessor, Ed Cahill, had been a roaring success as a dashing and articulate preacher. Cahill was not strong as a church builder, but was outspoken and vigorous in community work. His ministry attracted engineers from Lockheed and Ph.D.s from the Centers for Disease Control and Emory University.

When Pickett learned of the scientific makeup of the congregation, he felt intimidated and quickly shifted his very first sermon from the theme of science and religion to love. He was keenly uncomfortable with the standardized sermon talkbacks, where the congregation eagerly challenged the preacher on everything imaginable. Cahill had thrived on the talkbacks, which often lasted longer than the sermon itself.

With congregational expectations colliding with Pickett's strengths, the early going in Atlanta was rocky. Parishioners missed Cahill's explosive, dramatic style and natural tendency to confrontation. They were not experienced institutionalists and did not know to appreciate many of the things Pickett knew how to teach them. During the first year, parishioners figuratively sat back with their arms crossed waiting to see what this new guy on the block would do. Gene was never in danger of being fired, but it took about two years to win them over. Whereas Miami had been a teaching church and Richmond a supportive one, Atlanta furnished a cantankerous clan. During the course of Gene's ministry there the abrasive edges softened, and although different constituencies remained, they never became rivalrous. Atlanta blessedly evolved into a vibrant community of diverse tribes.

The church was situated in an old, second-hand building. Gene, an ever-observant minister, spent considerable time cleaning up the exterior and painting the floors and steps. People appreciated the fact that he willingly dirtied his hands and labored to beautify church premises that had been neglected.

Gene has always been conscious of and sensitive to aesthetic matters, but he is not sure where this came from. He started painting with oils as a child, trying to copy the works of the masters like Cezanne's "Still Life." His mother kept an orderly house and was concerned about attractive apparel, but Gene was the family member who was interested in how the house was furnished and appointed. In all of his churches he has intentionally created an attractive setting for worship, paying attention to details of flower and chair arrangements, and to the general decor of the room. Traveling to Unitarian Universalist fellowships in the South as the visiting preacher, Pickett was exasperated to see congregations worshiping in barren rooms within shabby premises.

Gene maintained a sensitive eye for beautiful art and collected sculpture, graphics, Transylvanian embroideries, and candlesticks. Every time the Pickett family moved into a new home, Helen and the three children would set up the beds and get the kitchen cleared to make peanut butter sandwiches. Meanwhile, Gene would be maneuvering things around in the living room, calling to his wife, "Helen, could you please come in here and see how you like this?" He would already be mounting pictures on the wall, first and foremost concerned about the aesthetic feeling of their new residence. Beauty and order were profoundly interwoven in his sensibilities.

Although Gene resisted building or moving to a new site in Richmond, it was clear from the outset that the Atlanta congregation would need to relocate. The church occupied a small city corner with limited parking capacity. Members were afraid to gather there for night meetings because of the need to park at a distance. When the Picketts arrived, a new location was the number one item on the church agenda.

The decision was soon made to sell the building and look for a place to erect a new church. The building would be hard to sell, since it stood in an unattractive area. Controversy arose when the initial offer to buy the structure came from the Black Muslims. The church agonized over the offer because of the so-called exclusionary tactics of the Muslims. Gene took the position that they should not sell to them because of their reverse prejudice, a judgment he is unsure he would make today. The Muslims were turned down in a tight, heated vote. Fortunately for church finances, an oil company was interested. They bought the corner lot, tore down the church, and built a gas station.

Not Standing Still

The Atlanta congregation needed nearly three years to find suitable property. Prospective neighbors regularly objected to them because they were an integrated congregation. During this period the church moved temporarily to a former elementary school where their worship services and church school were held. They also leased office and meeting space on nearby Peachtree Street. Surprisingly, during this protracted transitional time, church membership grew and enjoyed a productive program life. They worked with a design architect to enhance the barren school auditorium. Gene worked vigorously to cultivate lay leadership. He never got rid of the pulpit-pew talkbacks as he had hoped, but he became better at handling them and even started to appreciate the symbolic value of this cherished Atlanta custom.

Worship services were imaginative, employing dramatic readings by laity and the music of a gifted cellist member. With the purchase of a decent piano, Sunday morning musical offerings were expanded to include popular and folk music as well as classical. The most prominent vocalist to sing during worship services was Bernice Johnson Reagon. She occasionally attended the Atlanta Unitarian church, enrolling her young son in the church school. When she sang, her powerful voice required no accompaniment. She was filled with righteous rage as an African-American woman, and her music reflected this sensibility. Years later, before a General Assembly performance by Sweet Honey in the Rock, she and Gene mused about their changes in stature: Bernice had become a founding member and director of the famous singing ensemble that was about to perform, while Gene had ascended to the presidency of the UUA.

During this period in the interim facility, Gene greatly strengthened the congregation's pledge canvass and built a robust church infrastructure. These organizational foundations made possible the move from the inadequate school spaces to their own new building.

Because of its integrated membership, the church was unable to obtain required zoning on suitable property within

Atlanta's city limits. Fortunately, a church member who was the town planner for an adjacent county located an available piece of property along the expressway. The tract was costly and relatively small; they would have to cram everything they wanted onto two acres. Yet it was a highly visible and properly zoned location. They engaged an excellent architect in Atlanta to design the building, and with minimal debate about the cost involved, the church forged ahead. Everyone was enthralled with the proposed design: a circle in a square.

Circle in a Square

When the Catholic architect Joseph Amisano was alerted that preaching was important in the Unitarian Universalist tradition, he designed the pulpit, rather than an altar, as the focal point. An Atlanta newspaper described the modernistic sanctuary in this way: "The new Unitarian Universalist Church has a square-shaped exterior with 133-foot sides and features a stadium-style sanctuary. It is an award-winning structure which also houses seventeen classrooms, a social room, and a kitchen. The $460,000 buff-colored brick building has large plate glass windows with long strips of stained glass in the entrance.

"The circular sanctuary features off-white carpets and walls that blend with the light birch stained ceiling. The sanctuary seats are covered with orange-red cushions. The Reverend Mr. Pickett is excited about the new sanctuary arrangement. He said "it lessens the gap between the minister and the congregation, giving you a feeling of being closer to the people, of being a part of them rather than being set apart, talking with them, rather than at them."

Pickett found the sanctuary a comfortable space within which to preach, and its design accommodated a variety of desirable dramatic elements. The sanctuary became a setting for poetry readings, programs on the Theater of the Absurd and modern dance, concerts of original music, and exhibits by local painters and sculptors. Although the acoustics were superb, the sanctuary was also equipped with a solid sound system. It was a huge circle, but a few people could gather for an intimate wedding in the lower area, and with controlled lighting, feel perfectly comfortable. It was like a giant living room with the capacity to engage all the faces of a faith family.

Pickett fully employed the lay resources and liturgical equipment at his disposal. He was glad to share worship responsibilities with laity, recruiting a vigorous crew of volunteers to assist him in worship planning and execution, selecting flowers, dances, drama, and music in a varied and animating way. There was no formal worship committee, so Gene apportioned the tasks and remained in overall control of the Sunday morning liturgy.

Gene delighted in being the choreographer for each worship experience, developing an intricate scheme of lighting, usually staffed by high school youth at the control panel behind him. In fact, when his successors would ask his counsel, he would respond with particulars, such as, "Pay special attention to the subtleties of light and sound in the sanctuary." Gene adds, "I am not certain I was ever able to make very clear what I meant. I think I usually ended up giving the impression of being overly compulsive about petty details, which I was." His instruction sheets were so detailed they even specified that Helen left during the offering after singing with her autoharp!

Sermon writing was still accomplished on late Saturday nights and early Sunday mornings and continued to be a burden. Congregational life grew so complicated and intense that partly out of desire, and partly out of desperation, Gene in later years preached only twice a month. In addition, one special service per month required inordinate effort, but was never as laborious as composing a sermon. Guest speakers filled the pulpit on remaining Sundays. One of the favorite participational services held each year was a "Zorba the Greek Sunday," which eventually expanded to include a breakfast, dancers, bouzouki players, and weekend-long festivities. There was no Sunday off in the contract of ministers in that era, so Gene was involved every Sunday in one fashion or another.

Gene and Toby

For a church of its size and complexity, the Unitarian Universalist Congregation of Atlanta was deplorably understaffed. In addition to Gene as senior minister, Kay Hoffman worked for years as director of religious education. Later, Toby Van Buren joined the staff as an assistant minister with special responsibility for the 150 youth. Lamentably, Toby, though young and attractive himself, later confided in Gene that he was actually frightened to death of the youth. When the Atlanta church went to three worship services and sponsored the Northwest Congregation, Gene would preach two services at the home church, and Toby would deliver one at the other church at the same time. The following Sunday they would preach the same sermons at the other location. In this way they staffed three services a Sunday for a year. During Pickett's tenure in Atlanta the church also seeded two additional congregations and now, there are half a dozen more. Gene and Toby enjoyed working together, although they were markedly different in style and temperament, and wrangled over many an idea. Gene had to pick up after Toby when he caused a ruckus, like the time he used the word "fuck" from the church pulpit.

Helen was sitting in a worship service one Sunday when she heard a congregant behind her describe both Gene and Toby to a visitor: "Now that young one, he's the liberal, and the other one, the older guy, is academic and stodgy." Helen did not turn around and offer a firm rebuttal, but she thought to herself that the reason Toby could be an upstart was because Gene, a true liberal, supported Toby's behavior, then stood accountable for the fallout. Even though there were tensions, both ministers were invested in the relationship, so they started visiting a psychiatrist to resolve the differences in their working styles.

The bond between Gene, the incorrigible institutionalist, and Toby, the unfettered spirit, echoes a story told about Stan Kenton, the jazz musician. Kenton responded brusquely to a frustrated young band member who was tired of all the scut work and boring travel required of a professional performer. Kenton said, "Hey, quit whining, remember you aren't paid for blowing your saxophone. You are primarily paid for making the bus rides!" Toby disliked making all those "bus rides" to undergird a well-functioning religious community. He stayed two years, then went to Baton Rouge, Louisiana, and later, Beverly, Massachusetts. Because Toby liked fishing as much as being a cleric, he ultimately quit the ministry and went into commercial fishing.

In a profound sense, Gene was simultaneously a conservative, a radical, and a liberal. He was a conservative in that he was a diehard institutionalist, interested in preserving the values and visions of Unitarian Universalism in each of his congregations. He was a radical because he went to the root of issues and needs. And most of all, he was a liberal because he was generous of heart, magnanimous in sharing power, and tolerant of significant differences.

Adult Education Flourishes

Worship was not the only dimension of church life that blossomed in Atlanta. The adult education program, run by lay volunteers and overseen by the senior minister, drew 300 to 400 people per night, four nights a week, to the twenty-five to thirty different classes offered each period. With three terms per year and many hundreds of participants each term, the adult education program was the largest of its kind anywhere in the city. It offered courses in personal growth, skills development, and theological study.

Abounding with competent social service professionals, the Atlanta church developed intensive, interpersonal relations groups. These well-trained facilitators led groups of eight persons through a tightly structured, book-oriented process of encounter and discovery. These programs both attracted new members and strengthened the fabric of the Atlanta congregation.

This was a period of numerous divorces in the congregation, and the staff responded with "transitional groups" to support people during these crises. Gene was on the church premises every night; and, although seldom directly involved in the adult programs, he visited with people during the coffee break, reminding participants by his presence that this was a religious community and that the spiritual leader was "home" and cared about "his family and guests."

Quest for Racial Justice

The dominant social justice issue in the South continued to be race relations. Georgia liberals viewed the Alabama state line as "the border," feeling considerably safer in their own state than in the neighboring one. When attending a district meeting in Alabama, they would remark, "Well, we're crossing the border now," and would drive with some trepidation. The racial confrontation in Selma, Alabama, occurred during Pickett's ministry in Atlanta.

In 1965, Selma became a flashpoint in the fight to register blacks to vote in the South. In response to Martin Luther King's call, thousands gathered from across the nation to take part in a march to Montgomery. The peaceful march was brutally attacked and turned back by local police and state troopers, and in the aftermath, Unitarian Universalist minister James Reeb was murdered on the streets of Selma. Pickett participated in this march, and during this volatile time both the Picketts' home and the Atlanta church served as stations of hospitality for Unitarian Universalist ministers from all parts of the country.

The children of Coretta and Martin Luther King, Jr., were the first to integrate the elementary school that the Pickett girls attended, so Gene and Helen grew personally acquainted with the King family. King's dentist was a civil rights activist and a member of the Atlanta Unitarian Universalist church. Martin Luther King, Jr., occasionally preached there, as did his father, "Daddy" King, who would bring his splendid choir with him. Coretta King occasionally consulted with Gene about her children's experiences in the newly integrated school. Later, when Gene was UUA president, he met Coretta again in Washington, DC, at a White House gathering and was simply affected that Coretta even remembered him.

The Atlanta congregation felt guilty about moving outside of the central city, so they decided to start a Unitarian Universalist fellowship and a child-care center in the African-American neighborhood they had previously vacated. Earlier, the Unitarian Universalist Service Committee had helped found and continued to sponsor an inter-racial Council on Human Relations, an organization staffed by a member of the Atlanta congregation. The church continued to boycott business enterprises that failed to integrate. Members were equally embroiled in the Save Our Public Schools drives in Atlanta.

Although the Atlanta congregation had African-American members, it never became highly integrated. Atlanta already possessed its share of liberal black churches with ministers like Andrew Young. There was also a progressive African-American Baptist church, whose pastor had received his

Ph.D. from the University of Chicago. These congregations naturally attracted the majority of the open-minded, activist blacks in the area. During the Pickett ministry in Atlanta, there was a painful clash between the activists for integration and the black power advocates for separation. Many whites in the Unitarian Universalist Congregation of Atlanta reacted negatively to the rise of the Black Power movement, both in the country and in the Unitarian Universalist Association, because they felt they were no longer needed.

Gene recounts a purported incident that illustrates his commitment to racial justice more as an adamant institutionalist than as a fiery prophet: "During the civil rights days in Georgia, two of my colleagues from the North had gotten themselves thrown in jail on some trumped-up charges, and I was called in the middle of the night to bail them out. When I arrived at the jail, my colleagues, thinking I suppose, to imitate Thoreau, inquired of me with much fanfare as to what I was doing free from prison when righteousness had prompted their incarceration. 'You want to know what I'm doing out here?' I am supposed to have replied: 'Getting damn fools like you out of there!'

"Well, to tell the truth, I have no memory whatsoever of this little incident and have a sneaking suspicion it is apocryphal. But I like it nonetheless, because it depicts me in the role of an institutionalist, which is what I am. I have marched in enough demonstrations to know what it means to be in the thick of the action, but that action is effective only if it is coupled with the ongoing support of a binded community—some mechanism for releasing damn fools from prison."

Public and Private Crises

This was also the time of the Vietnam War, and the Unitarian Universalist Congregation of Atlanta provided a rallying center for conscientious objectors and assistance to young men in their exodus to Canada. Gene preached consistently against the war and urged the United States to get out of Southeast Asia reasonably and peacefully. While engaging in dissent, he was able to be supportive of opposing views. During one of his many sermons on Vietnam he invited the president of the Atlanta congregation, who supported the war, to give his views during a worship service. Despite their opposing opinions on the war, they remained good friends.

Throughout Gene's ministries, he demonstrated an unerring ability to create a forum spacious enough to house diverse perspectives, even lively dissent, without allowing differences to threaten the overall religious community. His was not a bully pulpit, but a shared platform. Helen remembers that Gene's sermons had a direct effect on parishioners' thinking about the Vietnam War and many other socio-ethical issues, but Gene, true to his modest nature, would demur saying, "I'm never sure whether any sermons, especially mine, have much effect on the growth of members."

In addition to his newsletter "musings" and sermons, Pickett occasionally used the vehicle of the "Pastoral Letter" to communicate with his congregation on complex, often contentious, issues. He was particularly concerned with the growing impulsiveness of church members to press for votes on social issues during Sunday mornings: "There is a great deal more to a liberal religious institution than social action.

We should be highly selective in choosing the issues on which we take a public stand. Furthermore, any public stand we take should be made in accordance with the democratic procedures as stated in our church constitution and by-laws. All sides of an issue should be thoroughly discussed and understood, and when a vote is finally taken, full account should be taken of a minority point of view. Such matters should be considered at a duly called meeting of the congregation with every member being informed of the matters to be considered.

"It is on this very point that we get into difficulty with trying to take congregational action during the discussion period on Sunday mornings. The Sunday morning congregation is not a congregational meeting. On Sunday mornings let our Public Issues Committee inform those attending the service of vital social and political issues to be faced by them as individuals rather than pushing for votes.

"I am convinced that passing resolutions is frequently an easy way out—a safe way to avoid becoming personally involved in doing something about things we say we believe in. I am not interested in our becoming known as The Little Church With the Big Mouth. I am interested that we be personally confronted with the vital social and ethical issues of our community, that we become knowledgeable about them, and that we accept responsibility for putting our religious beliefs and convictions into practice."

In the years before *Roe* v. *Wade*, Gene was one of the few ministers in Atlanta involved in therapeutic abortion counseling and in assisting women to travel as far as Mexico City to receive abortions. In addition, he was active on the board of Planned Parenthood of Atlanta from 1965 to 1974. All of these social education, witness, and action involvements were time-consuming. Although Don Jacobsen, who succeeded Toby Van Buren as assistant minister and was responsible for religious education, participated in certain inreach and outreach ventures, Gene shouldered the brunt of prophetic witness.

Because of the tremendous personal counseling load associated with such a large congregation, Gene alone could not handle all of the requests. To respond to the need, he recruited eight therapists in the congregation and established a special ministerial counseling center. The counselee would first meet with the minister for one session, then with one of the designated volunteer therapists for three sessions, followed by an outside professional referral if necessary. Gene consulted with the counselors once a month, reviewing all the cases and determining whether someone should come back to him or go to somebody else. This system provided an important service to parishioners in crisis, but still proved draining to Pickett.

Gene also did extensive premarital counseling, scheduled on an hourly basis, and would sometimes perform as many as eight or nine weddings on a Saturday. Given the relatively young age of church members, Gene did not officiate at many memorial services, but because death was a singularly significant passage to him, he expended immense effort whenever a congregant died. The consummate caregiver, Gene would concur with the sentiment voiced in *Death of a Salesman*, that "attention must be paid" to everyone. His memorials were keenly responsive and individually sculpted.

Ed Mangiafico had joined the Atlanta church in 1958 during Ed Cahill's ministry, but he and his wife Jean grew increasingly involved during Pickett's "intellectually stimulating and emotionally responsive" pastorate. Mangiafico, a highly successful business leader, has continued his association with various UU societies throughout the continent, and the two families have remained close to this day. Mangiafico is particularly admiring of Pickett's organizational skills as a forceful yet caring religious leader. He describes Pickett as a consummate community-builder during a tumultuous period in twentieth-century Southern life that was filled with racial strife, adolescent rebellion, and the Vietnam War.

"He was a stable, centering presence amid the rampant divisiveness in Atlanta," says Mangiafico. "What he showed us as a religious leader, I have since tried to implement in my transactions in the business world. Gene Pickett taught me to gel the most extreme of individuals into a well-functioning team without blurring the divergent views and gifts of each player. He taught me to appreciate, not suppress, dissent. He didn't hide behind a shield of arrogance. He would challenge me and others into living *our* own chosen values.

"Perhaps his greatest genius as a leader, displayed in Atlanta and later in Boston, has been his heightened and uncanny sensitivity to human beings. He engages people directly and humanely, seeing into them at depths which the rest of us rarely visit."

Shaking Hands With the Devil

"In the midst of winter, I finally discovered that
there was in me an invincible summer."

ALBERT CAMUS

The King Grows Weary

Although not an image that Gene would choose for himself,
the Jungian archetype of the king certainly contains features
that resemble Pickett's ministerial leadership. The good
king, neither dictator nor weakling, is a generative man who
orders the entire realm, blessing and being blessed by the
inhabitants, enlivening the people to serve transcendent ideals that they hold in common. The description by Robert
Moore and Douglas Gillette, in *The King Within*, paints a suitable portrait of Pickett's leadership: "The king provides a
safe, containing space where the people around him can
flourish. He offers encouragement by taking care to really
see others. In beholding his fellows he mirrors and affirms
them. He confirms their individuality and the reality of their
suffering and their joy. He blesses their lives by sanctifying
the fruits of their inner and outer labors."

Jungian therapists would also sagely note that in dysfunctional families like Gene's, in which there is an immature, weak, or absent father and the king energy is inadequately available, the tribal unit is usually given over to disorder and chaos. Some children of such family systems never fully survive the traumatic, tenacious stranglehold. Others, like Gene Pickett, although suffering deep and permanent wounds, are able, through grit and grace, to convert their blighted childhood into a triumphant adulthood. Michael Meade in speaking of kingly power describes the transformation as follows in his book, *Men and the Water of Life*:

"The king has blessed the same place that the father cursed. The father bit the son's head off; the king anoints his head. Where the father can't help but open a wound, the king is able to place a blessing. One source of the word *bless* comes from the French, *blessure*, which means wound. One of the responsibilities of those who would rule, lead, or mentor becomes learning to see into the wounded area of others and spot the blessed streak that suffered the wound."

As time progressed, Gene could not sustain the kingly presence he had established in Atlanta. The realm was thriving, but the king was faltering. Gene was never a tyrant, even a benevolent one, but he was the governor of his church domain and was reluctant to let power out of his hands. Gene acknowledges that this need to maintain control finally overwhelmed him and damaged his family. He was driven to prove himself, hopeful that his work ethic could dismantle the impostor syndrome that gnawed away at his psyche. It was a fruitless quest. He had become a desperate workaholic.

Matters were complicated by his inability to press for needed staff support. During Gene's ministry, the church never had a full-time custodian. He felt pity for the parish because it struggled so hard to meet its financial goals, and he was hesitant to push them any further.

Atlanta did have a church administrator, and Pickett had a personal secretary to help with appointments, but since he still wanted to oversee how everything was handled, the details eventually overwhelmed him. When his mother needed him as a child, he responded affirmatively, unable to establish firm boundaries between his personal needs and hers. Furthermore, recalling the time when A. Powell Davies saw Gene for only twenty minutes, Pickett vowed that he, unlike Davies, would always have ample time for his parishioners. The fact that he was available for everyone proved both a blessing and a curse.

Gene never took a regular day off during his entire parish ministry career. He could not let go of the controls, even for a day, lest the empire crumble and his weaknesses be exposed. Periodically, Helen would calculate how long it had been since Gene was home for an evening together. She resented a number of aspects of his ministry, but none more than the fact that he had no time for his family. He would work extra hard to certify his value, but it was a fruitless effort, since gaining one's full worth through work is impossible.

Proving Oneself

Gene was caught in a self-defeating trap: he was beloved and effective in serving the largest congregation in our Association, but his emotional health was caving in and his family bonds were unraveling. As he disconsolately states, "At this point in my accelerating descent, more important than family, than anything, was my compulsion to prove myself as a minister!"

Helen knew that Gene was both responsible for his workaholism and helplessly tangled in its grasp. "I knew that he couldn't help himself, he was hanging on by his fingernails, but it was very, very hard on us. So he attended committee meetings every night, and then went out with interested parishioners to drink beer afterwards. He arrived home after 1:00 A.M. every night." Helen went to bed early to get up with the children, so she would see Gene only for a rushed breakfast. They would sit and talk for a half-hour, then Gene would bound off to the church to commence the vicious cycle all over again.

Helen recalls, "It was a long time before I realized I should just get Gene his own alarm clock. He would let me try to guess when he wanted to get up. Then he would rise and say, 'Why didn't you get me up at...?' A sick game. He would usually come home for dinner, but that was time spent with the children more than the two of us. There were periods when Gene was involved in Saving the Schools meetings and wasn't home for dinner twenty-one days in a row! I mean, that's how bad it was. I'm sorry, my love, but I was hanging on by my fingernails, too! You were driven by demons."

But Helen did not rebel or shout, "Enough is enough, I quit!" And when the children wondered, "Hey, Mom, where's Dad?," Helen covered for Gene with explanations about his work. Gene loved his three daughters and was affectionate with them, bathing and reading to them as youngsters when he was home. He just wasn't home very much. He never considered his presence on the domestic front to be critical. His own father had been an absentee parent, so Gene didn't know otherwise. He devalued his role as a father. During the week there was school, the other fathers were at work, and the kids and Helen did things together. But Saturdays were particularly frustrating and lonely, because the other Dads were home playing with their children and Gene was still off doing church work.

Gene counted on Helen to remain a reliable, impervious rock amidst the exhausting whirlwind of his professional life. He simply couldn't conceive that she might need him as much as she did. He saw her as being self-sufficient, possessing boundless energy as both homemaker and mother. Yet Helen would feel overwhelmed, falling into a depression that made such capability impossible. This state drew no sympathy from Gene. He never wanted to see Helen tired, because he needed her to "bear up" through thick and thin. He didn't believe that his wife, on whom he counted to be his fortress, might be crumbling herself.

"Now if he had shut me out completely, I don't think I could have stood it," says Helen. "But I knew Gene needed me in his work life for moral support and parish involvement, and I drew value from all of that. I contributed to our problem by trying 'not to need Gene,' not to make demands so he could be free for all of those others who supposedly needed him more than I did! That was a great mistake."

From time to time Helen would plead for Gene to take a relaxing day off, but he was unprepared to hear it, let alone seize it. And Helen would sometimes wonder, "Do I have to threaten to leave Gene for him to listen to me? But I decided I wasn't going to do that, because I wasn't sure I wanted to or even could. I wasn't about to threaten something I wasn't able to carry out. I had very deep insecurities of my own, and divorce was a dirty, unthinkable word in my family; and when my sister Julia got divorced, my father never got over it. I thought about divorce, but I couldn't even picture myself doing that successfully. Plus I still believed in Gene. I was his number one fan, and people admired the two of us as a successful public team in the church. But an edge of bitterness was creeping into my heart, because the church was getting all of his attention, time, and energy. Furthermore, Gene was getting the accolades and good feedback while I was barely holding on, trying to keep family life operating by myself. I joined him on his territory of church functions and a heavy social life, but I felt he didn't join the children and me on our territory."

Gene and Helen were very responsive to the call of duty and to other people's needs, but both had difficulty assuring that their own personal needs were met. Helen considers that not being allowed to make any significant decisions while growing up accentuated her marital submissiveness. She had learned to accept whatever happened to her and tended to feel that she had no power to change things.

She recounts an example of this powerlessness: "On Thanksgiving Day I was busy cooking the turkey dinner, and Gene became somewhat impatient because I didn't have time to help him get the plastic sheeting tacked up on the screened porch in the face of the oncoming winter. The reason he was so intent on getting this job done on Thanksgiving Day was that this was the first day he had spent at home since Labor Day, and he didn't expect to have another day at home before Christmas Day. When the full impact of this hit me, I was furious, but, in order not to spoil the day, I choked it down.

"Over the years I had come to accept that Gene is a very private person, but I didn't realize the extent to which he was not sharing his uncertainties and anxieties with me. When he didn't talk much, I tended to feel (out of my own insecurities) that it was somehow my fault. I knew Gene loved and needed me, and I believed he meant well. I learned to make a little go a long way in terms of communication, affection, and private time together. But the two of us weren't going to be able to resolve our problems by ourselves. We needed help."

Gene, utterly buried in his career, was oblivious to the magnitude of Helen's desperation. "I just felt that I was never on top of the church work, and that any time I took off from it was dangerous. Even if I had heard Helen's cry, I don't think I could have done anything about it, because I was absolutely lost in workaholism for my very own sense of survival."

Divorce Is Broached

One summer day, feeling completely inadequate as both father and husband, Gene broached the subject of divorce with Helen, strictly from the perspective of his own unworthiness. He exclaimed, "Helen, don't you think you would be better off without me? If you choose to leave me, I'll fully understand!" What he was saying in typical self-deprecating fashion was: "I'm in such terrible shape. You don't need to put up with me any more, Helen, if you don't want to."

His confession was a rare gift of self-disclosure, and Helen realized just how dreadful Gene was feeling. He had been so noncommittal and inexpressive about his emotional despair during their fifteen years of marriage that she had resigned herself to this pattern. Helen knew that Gene depended on her; the problem was not that she was extraneous, but, rather, that he was so emotionally closed. Gene was not trying to get rid of Helen, but he didn't know how she could tolerate his workaholism any longer. Blaming himself, he was willing to have her leave the marriage. The truth was that Helen didn't want Gene *out* of her life, but *in* her life.

Outwardly, Gene and Helen looked marvelous; inwardly their partnership was dying. It took six years of collaborative commitment to in-depth therapy to save their marriage. Upon returning to Atlanta in 1986 to become the church's minister emeritus, Gene candidly recalls their marital anguish in a moving address: "I have struggled with the triangular relationship between minister, family, and congregation for almost all of my ministry. Helen, as the daughter of a minister, thought she knew all the pitfalls and perils of parsonage life. In the glow of newfound love, we were confident that we could handle any problem. But the church is a seductive lover for a new, young minister (and often for a middle-aged, experienced minister as well).

"To prove myself worthy and lovable to my congregations required such time and energy, that it is nothing short of a miracle that our marriage survived. Remembering the misunderstanding and the anger, the forgiving and the new beginnings of those years still causes me deep anguish. . . . Looking back, it is painful to realize how much of the responsibility for this unbalanced relationship rested with me. I did not take seriously that I was a person first, with wife and children, and then a minister. It was I, not you the church, who created unreasonable expectations."

Except for Saturday nights when Gene was writing his sermon and unavailable, the Picketts would schedule dinner and party engagements with parishioners unless, of course, there were business meetings. They were both popular socially and responded to every conceivable invitation. Ironically, Gene, by nature an extremely private person, was involved with people day and night. As he later observed, "I think being an introvert trying to act like an extrovert made my parish ministry doubly draining rather than energizing."

Unable to prevail on Gene to alter his work habits, Helen would hold on to her own sanity all year long just waiting for their vacation. In theory, Gene had a month off and a month on call, but he wouldn't surrender that much time. One summer during the grueling Atlanta years, the Picketts had planned an unusually long vacation—two weeks in the mountains and two weeks at the beach—and at the last minute Gene had to do a memorial service. Helen and the children were literally sitting in the living room waiting for Father to come home and get in the car.

When Gene finally got away on this summer journey with the family, the vacation proved far too long. He suffered withdrawal pains from his work addiction and was eager to get home to feed his obsession. Helen would often say, "Gene, you need a vacation," when she really meant, "I need a vacation with you." In any case, they were unable to find a mutually gratifying way to get eleven months of living and loving into one month. One time in therapy Helen contended that Gene was emotionally crippled and simply didn't have the capacity to give affection and time to his family. The therapist shot back, "Not true, all those people at the church are getting his attention!" Gene was empowering to parishioners, yet unable either to nourish his being or enjoy his family.

Marital Therapy

For the most part Gene maintained a good public front to cover his emotional and marital turmoil. But mid-way through 1965, he began to unravel psychologically and became almost nonfunctioning. In desolation Pickett summoned two psychologists who were members of the congregation and confided, "I'm at my wit's end. I don't know if I can go on. I need help right away. What do you suggest?"

Gene explained that he didn't want to participate in the orthodox psychoanalysis that he had previously undergone. Both friends declined to be Gene's therapist and recommended an outside psychiatrist, Sidney Isenberg, who specialized in counseling ministers and social workers. It was Gene's contention that "if I could just get myself straightened out, my marriage would straighten itself out as well."

So Gene participated in therapy every week for a year, and Isenberg diagnosed Pickett's presenting problem as triangular—the church, Gene, and Helen. He thought that Helen should enter the therapeutic process, a suggestion that she welcomed. Helen had never been in either therapy or analysis, yet earlier, when she knew she wasn't coping well within the marriage, she had expressed interest in seeing a professional. However, because Gene was invested in perceiving Helen as his hale and happy mate, he discouraged the idea.

Isenberg, unlike Gene's psychoanalyst during his Meadville days, was familiar with and sympathetic to religious institutions, so he helped the Picketts sort out their congregational gridlock. In the fall of 1966 they joined forces in therapy, and Helen felt personally invited into Gene's inner world of turmoil. Rarely did either of them see Isenberg alone during their six-year marital rehabilitation process. The focus of therapy was primarily on their relationship, but as their marriage started to heal, Isenberg helped them confront the problems inherent in the other leg of the triangle, the church.

During the depths of the therapy process, the Picketts had to "shake hands with the devil" on more than one occasion. There were plenty of tears and thin times during this reconstructive emotional and relational journey. Helen would experience crying jags, and daughter Ann, who was about nine years old, would observe, "Mama, maybe you need to see a psychiatrist!" Little did she know.

The girls were not told about the therapy; neither was the church, although their coterie of close friends knew. The healthier the Picketts became, the more willing they were to convey how transformative in-depth therapy had proven for them. In his pastoral counseling, Gene would use the insights gained from his own, hard-won personal growth. The psychologically oriented congregation was very understanding.

An Atlanta sermon on November 13, 1966 describes in general terms what the Picketts were valiantly trying to embody in their own lives: "My main point is that in a marriage neither partner should be in a constant or consistent position of dominance or subservience. Both partners have need to be themselves, to be real persons worthy of respect and love. Love based on a feeling of equality and translated into cooperation is something that takes time and effort to build. We must build and rebuild this love relationship, for love does not sustain itself unaided. Successful marriage is the result of hard work, real understanding, the ability to communicate in terms of thoughts and feelings, and a continued willingness to cooperate."

A Changed Man and Woman

By the end of their arduous therapy in 1972, Gene was becoming less depressed: in his own words, "a different man." He sometimes even chose to stay home for entire afternoons following their 11:00 A.M. therapy sessions. A significant lesson for Gene was that he could stop trying to validate his worth at the church all the time. Slowly but surely, he loosened his iron-tight squeeze on work.

He realized the crucial importance of his family bonds, which had "really gone to pot." Gene knew he had neglected Helen but seldom considered that the children were suffering, too, although for special events like the girls' recitals or plays at school, Helen had always booked them on Gene's schedule so he would not fail to appear.

All of the girls missed their father during their formative years. The oldest daughter, Ann, although claiming today that she felt full assurance of her father's love as a child, still bemoans his visible absence from the home front. Their summer vacations furnished islands of relief and renewal, because the family would be safely tucked away in a car—void of phones, pressures, and parishioners. Summer treks with the family were filled with games, adventures, and delightful projects. "At last," Ann remembers, "we girls had our parents' undivided attention!"

The youngest daughter, Emily, has no visual memory of her father before her teenage years. She forged her sense of identity and happiness essentially outside the Pickett family context.

Like her oldest sister Ann, Emily has since formed strong ties with her father. During her first year of college, Gene wrote personal letters to Emily, full of news and warmth. This unsolicited gesture of concern and caring touched Emily. At the tender age of seventeen, with the reluctant approval of her parents, she left home to work and live on her own and eventually return to college. Since that time, Emily has been able to meet her parents pretty much as equals. "They are currently my best friends who help me through tough times and whose company I immensely enjoy!" Emily contends that she combines both her father's introverted temperament and her mother's chastened buoyancy. "Proudly, I am a blend of Mama and Papa!"

The middle daughter, Martha, also felt the complex influence of her father on her life: "During the Atlanta years, most of what I knew about Papa I learned from Mama. She talked about what a great minister he was and how well-loved by the congregation. I admired him a great deal, yet somewhat from a distance, because I didn't know him so much as I knew *about* him.

"Papa worked all the time, seven days a week, twenty-four hours a day. The exception was summertime, when he became a different person. Every summer Papa had a special project. One year it was macramé. I still cherish the belt I made. Papa also developed a family reputation regarding picnics. He had a knack for selecting hostile environments. I have memories of picnicking in mountain fog or on wind-swept, rocky beaches.

"I give both my parents full credit for creating in me a strong conscience and a powerful sensitivity to injustice. Papa also had a tremendous influence on my faith, even though he didn't discuss his personal beliefs with me."

When Martha worked as a director of religious education at Second Unitarian Universalist Church of Chicago in the early 1980s, Gene attended one Sunday and listened to his daughter deliver a cogent and stirring sermon. He was moved to tears. During the coffee hour after the service, Martha was avalanched with praise and ensconced in satisfying conversations. Gene grew increasingly restless and was ready to leave. When he approached his daughter, she gently chided him, "Papa, we were always the last family to leave the Atlanta church. Today, the situation is reversed; you are Martha's father, and you will wait until this preacher is ready to depart!"

Before their sustained therapy, Helen had resisted making demands on Gene as his wife and the mother of their children, because she knew other people needed him as well. Yet in downplaying the primacy of family needs, her own sense of worth plummeted. In therapy Helen learned to disentangle herself from the vicious triangle and grow more assertive. The consummate gift Helen received in this intensive therapy process was to have Gene open his heart full of anguish to her.

Helen also realized as a result of the therapy that "while being totally committed to our marriage, I finally felt free within the marriage, as compared with my former feelings of being bound by Gene's and my own unreasonable expectations. Gene could now count on me, but he couldn't take me for granted! The other satisfying change has been our new level of communication. We now trust each other with our weaknesses and vulnerabilities as well as with our strengths; we understand each other so well; and each of us is the other's best friend. Nonetheless, we still heartily agree with the sentiment: 'we have never found an issue so trivial it is not worth a bicker!'"

The Picketts had lived in Atlanta for ten years, and it was time to consider a sabbatical. Gene had previously avoided them like the plague because he did not want to lose church command. Whenever publicity about professional sabbaticals arrived in the mail, Gene would hide it. Yet, when church leaders recommended that they put a new roof on the church in honor of his tenth anniversary in Atlanta, Gene surprised everyone, especially Helen, by offering the counter-proposal of a sabbatical. The Atlanta church warmed up to the idea. Gene did not want to study during his leave, and luckily, the board of trustees considered relaxation and renewal sufficient reasons for taking a sabbatical. The board offered five months of the church year, plus two months of summer, for the whole family to get away.

The church raised money for the Picketts' round-trip airfare to Europe where they could live on Gene's salary during their travels. The Picketts rented a house for three months in England, so the girls, who were eleven, thirteen, and fifteen, could settle in and have access to a library when they were not sightseeing. The family also spent time in Portugal,

Spain, France, Holland, Germany, and Switzerland. Then the girls flew back home to their grandmother and Gene and Helen took a final tour, led by Dana and Debbie Greeley, to Transylvanian Unitarian churches. In addition to Gene's intrepid move of asking for this travel sabbatical, he was even able to be relaxed enough in Europe to travel without making any hotel reservations except for the first two nights. He was a changed man, or at least changing!

Upon returning to the Atlanta church, the challenge was clear: could Gene exercise a balanced life between his professional and family obligations? Given the staff realities in Atlanta, could this large church thrive without his old patterns of omnipresent leadership? He came to the painful realization that he still had a tiger by the tail in Atlanta and that he could not harness it. He could not remain the senior minister in Atlanta. He did not want or need to prove himself anymore. During his final two years in the Atlanta church, Gene's mind moved on while his body prepared for a shift as well.

He contemplated taking a smaller, less complicated church that paid an adequate salary. He had also been contacted by UUA President Robert Nelson West earlier in his Atlanta years about assuming a post at the UUA, but none of the available positions seemed appropriate. Finally, when the Scovel Commission recommended that there be a post in the Department of Ministry specifically concerned with theological education, Gene was called. It sounded like an interesting job and the right match. He would not have to do fundraising, and he was fond of both Bob West and David Pohl, under whom he would be directly working. The one drawback was that he would have to take a twenty percent cut in pay.

Called to Boston

"O God, who in the midst of life dost bring us to an awareness of the smallness of our individual selves, grant us to know that the mark we leave will depend more on our grasp than our height, more on our vision than our weight—that our true measure lies in the depth of our affections and the endurance of our graciousness."

PAUL CARNES

Fresh Posts

The Picketts loved Atlanta, but the decision that made emotional and vocational sense at this time was to move on. Gene envisioned that smaller churches like Lexington and Baltimore, where he precandidated but was not chosen, would generate less pressure than Atlanta. Yet even in the tiniest of congregations, there would still be onerous sermon preparation. The nine-to-five working hours of an Association official would furnish Gene with the family time he so desperately desired. In weighing all the factors, it seemed advisable to take the drop in salary and migrate to Boston.

Helen would have to find work, but she was ready and

willing. Past forty years of age, Helen entered the job market not just from economic necessity. She was eager to try something new. With one year of high-school typing and no experience with a modern electric typewriter, Helen practiced some, learned to operate the hold button on an office telephone, and sought a job.

Before long, she was hired by Wellesley College, which was committed to employing women who, like Helen, possessed potential but lacked experience. She was not at all offended to be asked, "Do you type?". Within a year she became assistant to the Foreign Student Advisor, a fascinating position that included handling the immigration work for foreign students and faculty, counseling students on immigration problems, helping to run an international student center, and writing and distributing a weekly newsletter. During this period Helen also became deeply involved in the Cecilia Society, Boston's second-oldest choral group, of which she served as president for two years. She worked at Wellesley for five years, then left to "stand by my man" when he was appointed president.

Gene's first administrative job at the UUA was not as interesting as he had hoped, but his way of life was considerably more relaxed. The move, however, proved traumatic for the daughters, and especially unsettling to the two younger ones, Emily and Martha, who were in the ninth and eleventh grades. The oldest daughter, Ann, returned south to attend Guilford College, a Quaker school in North Carolina, but the high schoolers became depressed as a result of the transition.

The move to the Boston area enabled Ann to rebuild the

connection with her father, and she feels a strong identification with Gene, whom she finds to be a caring, quiet, nonjudgmental man, the very kind she has always admired and been attracted to. She is particularly proud that they share the same, rather unusual, Myers-Briggs profile (INFJ). As Ann triumphantly notes, "Our father-daughter bond today proves that it is never too late to restore a damaged relationship!"

Emily was deeply angry that her parents disrupted her satisfying life in Atlanta by moving the family north. Upon moving to Needham, Massachusetts, Emily was "initially stunned to see this stranger, my Dad, home for dinner!"

Yet the change was so important for Gene as a professional and for the Picketts as a couple that they simply had to make it work. Their health was at stake. Daughter Martha was later asked by her parents, "Why didn't you tell us how you were really feeling?" And she wistfully replied, "I knew I didn't want to move, but I also knew how important it was for the two of you."

Martha admires the extensive emotional and relational work her parents have done over the years. She recalls, "When I compare the Atlanta with the Boston years, it's like night and day. Mama and Papa have grown, both individually and together, in wonderful ways. Their genuine enjoyment of and respect for each other is a pleasure to witness."

In describing himself as a professional minister, Gene considered his pastoral gifts as paramount, his talents as an organizer and institutionalist second, his prophetic outreach next, with the roles of preacher and scholar holding down the cellar. Even during his substantial tenure as a UUA administrator he related to the staff as a pastoral presence. Pickett was proud of the bonds he formed with seminary students during his beginning post at the UUA. In this new position he made contact with theological students on behalf of the UUA, and he could tell immediately what a positive difference it made in their relating to the Association. In fact, some of these students were later among the first people to suggest that Gene run for the presidency. They liked his kindly manner and respected his integrity. Remembering his own seminary days when Wallace Robbins and A. Powell Davies had remained detached from students, Gene was committed to forging lively connections with the new generation of prospects entering parish ministry.

Pickett would later write about his efforts to enhance the internship program: "The Scovel Commission recommended, among other things, that the schools put more emphasis on the practical aspects of ministry and stressed the need for a well-structured internship program. They also stressed the importance of continuing education opportunities for ministers. With a special grant from the Veatch Program, the Council contracted with Harvard's School of Education to develop a comprehensive internship program which would serve as a model for well-structured internships. The Council, working with the Alban Institute in Washington, DC, and the Career Development Institute in Wellesley, Massachusetts, also instituted career development and continuing education programs, of which the new ministry start-up seminars have been the most successful.

"Both Meadville/Lombard and Starr King were critical of the report and both were skeptical, if not antagonistic, toward the work of the new Council. A major area of contention was the fact that the Association provided little financial support for the schools. The Council was not funded adequately and so was limited in its ability to develop new programs and was unable to provide significant financial support for the schools.

"I realize that this broad-stroke treatment does not do justice to the depth and seriousness of the differences and discussions that took place at the time, but the important lesson for me, which was to play a part in my presidency, was that until the Association could provide significant financial support for the schools, the relationship with the schools would continue to be strained and the Association's influence minimal.

"My greatest satisfaction came from my work with the theological students. This was the first time in many years that there had been a staff person devoting full time to working with students and theological education. Working at headquarters makes abundantly clear how crucially important it is to have the support and commitment of professional leaders if we are to have an effective and vital Association. And it became obvious that the time to begin to establish a good relationship is while the students are in theological school. Nurturing the relationship between student and Association at this stage of their development offers the best assurance that the relationship will continue to deepen and grow over the years. I think this is proving to be the case."

There was great relief in the Pickett household shortly after their arrival in Boston. The change was radical. Helen and Gene had more time for one another and the family.

Gene felt less pressure to prove himself in ways burdensome and unnatural for him. Opening Sunday on the church calendar had always been the Sunday after Labor Day. Helen consistently dreaded the beginning of the fall season in the parish ministry because she felt she was losing Gene until the next summer. Gene had entered each new church year with excitement about its potentialities, but also with a high pitch of anxiety. Now they sat, on the Sunday after Labor Day, leisurely reading the newspaper in their breakfast room, and Gene smilingly mused, "I wonder if it's normal not to miss it at all?" They were to bask in this calmer state for years.

Working With Robert West

Robert and Nancy West had been members of the Richmond Church but had left for Starr King School for the Ministry the year that Gene and Helen Pickett arrived. The two families got to know one another when the Wests came home during school breaks. Bob had been in the insurance business before going off to seminary at the age of twenty-five with Nancy and their small children. After graduation, the Wests returned south to Knoxville where Bob served as minister. Bob and Gene became colleagues in the Southeastern ministers' group, and their respective families gathered for meals and, occasionally, for shared vacations. When Bob was running for UUA president, Gene was in Atlanta and served as his Southern campaign coordinator.

One of the stories circulating from this era was about Robert Jordan Ross, who, after serving as a Methodist minister, became a member of Gene's church in Atlanta. Soon thereafter, inspired by Gene's ministry, Ross became fellowshipped by the UUA and went to work in the Department of Ministry under Joseph Barth. Gene was at a ministers' meeting in New Orleans, and a cluster of clergy were drinking and joking. Bob West, who was campaigning at the time for the UUA presidency, was present at the table. Gene humorously quipped, "I'll vote for you, Bob, if you make me head of the Department of the Ministry!" Bob Ross immediately phoned back to Beacon Street to Barth, anxiously declaring that West was going to make Pickett head of Barth's department. Naturally, Gene was kidding, yet years later when he did assume that post, Barth, with tongue in cheek, chided his former apprentice, "So, this is what you had been planning all along!"

When Gene decided to work at the UUA, it was in the home stretch of West's tenure. He remarked, "Bob West was president during one of the most difficult periods in the life of the Association. He had to overcome tremendous obstacles to keep the Association solvent while keeping it operating—and it operated at a surprising degree of effectiveness."

Bob had become quite discouraged and counted the days until his presidency would conclude. Gene was an ally who was both supportive and critical. Knowing how isolated Bob felt, Gene maintained a close friendship with him.

For Gene, the shift from working essentially around the clock in Atlanta to being a nine-to-five person in Boston proved both a godsend and a jolt. Some new and interesting programs were instituted, like the Start-up Ministry project, but Gene was accustomed to a pressure-packed work station and had difficulty adjusting to the lighter routine.

After Gene had served a year in the theological education position, President West appointed him head of combined congregational and ministerial services. Under this administrative revisioning, Gene was asked to mesh and coordinate several departments, and he viewed this fresh challenge a good match with his administrative skills and energy level.

It was troublesome explaining the new organizational arrangement to folks in the field. Gene experienced overt rancor and animosity at many of the district and ministers' meetings he attended. Thin-skinned by nature, he would often absorb the bulk of the ministerial malice through painful stomachaches. Honorably representing the Association during this era was no easy feat, but Pickett did it effectively because he was adroit in both speaking the truth and understanding people's concerns. Gene gained respect and friendship from both clergy and laity across the continent.

Paul Carnes Becomes President

When the Picketts first came to Boston they envisioned a short professional transition. Gene realized how personnel changed with different administrations, so he planned a two- to four-year stretch at the UUA before the next president came on board.

The timing would be good for the Pickett girls, since, after three years in Boston, they would have graduated from high school. This block of time would also furnish Gene the opportunity to restore his emotional equilibrium and figure out what he wanted to do with the rest of his professional career. He planned to resume parish life, and jokingly said he would only take a church large enough to pay him a decent wage but with little potential for growth. The longer he worked in Boston, the less certain he was that he wanted to reenter the parish scene.

None of the three presidential contenders in 1977— Paul Carnes, Gordon McKeeman or Jack Mendelsohn— talked with the staff about their personnel plans, so there was considerable uneasiness around the office at 25 Beacon Street. Members of the executive staff, including Pickett, were poised to tender their resignations, but when Carnes was elected, he invited everyone to remain in place. At that point Gene was still considering the question of whether he wanted to stay or move on.

Gene reported directly to Robert Senghas as the executive vice president, and they did not always see eye-to-eye. Most of the difficulty derived from Senghas's manner. He would lecture Pickett like a schoolboy. On the positive side, he was exceedingly conscientious and competent. Senghas became the real administrator at the UUA, and Pickett was the staff person who generated and steered continental program life. Carnes also brought onto the staff the bright, young manager of Jack Mendelsohn's General Assembly campaign, William Schulz, to serve as head of the Social Responsibility Department.

The UUA board of trustees, trying to gain greater clout and authority, fought West in the closing years of his presidency. They instituted a zero-based budget process and spent hours poring over every line item. Carnes had been accustomed to the parish ministry where his voice and viewpoint held considerable sway. But the UUA board had wrested power from West, and they were not about to relinquish it to the next president. Consequently, Carnes had trouble getting his budget requests through the board.

In his farewell speech, Senghas bemoaned the fact that his job required too much "nay-saying." In 1987, when Gene was asked to deliver the Berry Street Essay, he reviewed the West-Senghas executive years in a favorable, yet balanced light. His description of Senghas's role was particularly insightful: "During this time Bob Senghas was Executive Vice President. He had recently come from successful ministries in Davis, California, and Wellesley Hills, Massachusetts. He was a very competent administrator and the principal and most trusted advisor to Bob West. It was a very difficult job with few rewards. He usually was the bearer of bad news and new regulations to the staff and the receiver of staff dissatisfactions and criticisms of the administration. The job seemed to call forth more of his legal background than his pastoral one. He had to cope with endless details, almost never had a chance to travel, and received few strokes and little appreciation." Senghas approached Gene with tears in his eyes and asked for a copy of the address. He felt vindicated.

It soon became evident that Carnes, who had been a prominent parish minister, did not fully understand the nature of the Association's operation. He assumed a heavy travel schedule to raise and enhance the visibility of the Association, but sometimes when Pickett would walk into his office, Carnes would be staring at the wall over an empty desk. He made no major changes in structure or program. It was unclear how much of Carnes's conduct of the presidency was due to the illness that would consume him.

Pickett did not develop a close relationship with Carnes, so he was never privy to his feelings or opinions. But it soon could be observed that Carnes was denying the severity of his spreading cancer. It was only during the last couple of months of his life that he was willing to say to his staff colleagues, "I'm not going to make it."

An Unlikely Run

During Pickett's interval as the ministerial education director, he had established relationships with a number of young Meadville seminary grads like Lee Barker, William Holway, Stephan Papa, David Phreaner, and William Schulz. This clan of colleagues began to encourage Gene to run for the presidency. "My first thoughts about running for the presidency of our Association were stimulated by jokes and fantasies shared with Bill Schulz over meals at the local pub, the Fatted Calf. I said I would never want to be president because I didn't like to write speeches or answer correspondence. He offered to do both, excluding sermons. But, seriously, it was Bill Schulz's urging, encouraging, and supporting that helped me across this particular Rubicon. But even that would not have been enough without the love and encouragement of Helen."

Schulz and Pickett had developed a close friendship working together on the staff. "Bill and I lucked on to one another," says Gene. "I was hungry for the kind of relationship that he provided. It was partly a father-son kind of bond, but he was really too strong to be a good son. So he was more a buddy—the first time I had a genuine buddy. We spent time together in a way that I had never done with another man. So I think that whereas Bill could manipulate me, he was also a very steady supporter spurring me on: 'Come on, Gene, you can do it' that would directly counter my 'I can't do this.' It was a very satisfying and fulfilling relationship for me."

Gene described how he began to move toward the idea of the presidency in his Berry Street Essay: "If I was going to run, it was important to be assured of Paul's support. In one of my conversations with him, I told him I was thinking of running for president if he was not going to run for a second term. He said he would do anything he could to help me and that we should coordinate the timing of our announcements to my best advantage. Then he added that not only was he not running for a second term, he wasn't certain he would even make it through the first term. This was in January 1979, and he died that March." The board's vote for a presidential replacement was scheduled for the following month.

In reflecting on his improbable path to becoming the chief executive officer of the UUA, Pickett wrote: "While I had known six of the leaders of our movement (four presidents and two general superintendents), Dana was the standard against which I irrationally tended to measure myself. I say 'irrationally' because we were so very different (almost opposite) in background, experience, psychological makeup, leadership style, and volume. Dana was what I thought a UUA president should look like, act like, and sound like. In 1958 John Haynes Holmes described Dana as being 'packaged' for the presidency of the AUA. I agree with Holmes, and when I measured myself against Dana I felt quite inadequate.

"On reading his book I was interested (and somewhat comforted) to learn that Dana felt his pedigree was inadequate for the job. He wrote, 'My father wasn't president of Harvard, and my grandfather hadn't been mayor of Boston as had been the case with Samuel A. Eliot, and I wasn't an Eliot anyway. I hadn't married a Foote, a daughter of King's Chapel, a daughter of the minister, and a niece of the Eliots, as had Louis C. Cornish. I wasn't the son of a Unitarian minister, and the grandson of one, and the nephew of one, and the grandnephew of one as Frederick May Eliot had been. These were my three predecessors. I was, to be sure, a fifth-generation Unitarian, and my father enjoyed recalling that his father, as a boy, sat in the pew in back of Henry Wadsworth Longfellow. My grandmother Greeley had spoken from the Arlington Street Church pulpit forty years before I did. I started attending the Annual Meetings of the Association at age 17.'

"In contrast, I was not born Unitarian or Universalist. Indeed I had never heard the words until I was in college. There had never been a minister of any variety in my family. I came from a relatively undistinguished family living in a rural village in Maryland. However, my uncle was an undertaker and my mother was a member of the state Republican Committee. I had a perfect record of attendance at Methodist Sunday school for ten years and was made Sunday school superintendent at the age of fourteen. And I never served a church in New England.

"Dana writes that in 1959 he did not seek the presidency

but that someone had to do the job and he was willing to be the victim. In contrast, I did seek the job. I wanted it, and I would have been very disappointed if the board of trustees had not appointed me to fill the vacancy created by Paul Carnes's untimely death.

"Why did I think I was qualified to do the job? Why did I seek it, especially since I had left Atlanta and parish ministry because I wanted to be in a less pressured and demanding situation? In order to deal with these questions, let me say a bit about *before* 25 Beacon Street.

"When we arrived in Atlanta in 1962, church membership was 300. Over the next twelve years we built a new building, the church grew to 1,150 members, and the average attendance on a Sunday morning was 850. This was in addition to the 200 who left and, with our aid and blessing, organized Atlanta's Northwest Congregation. Our church school had 800 students, and we enrolled annually 1,800 persons in our adult education program. We had over forty committees and groups and, being both compulsive and controlling, I felt guilty if I didn't attend all of their meetings.

"During those years my attention and energy were focused primarily on my church and community. I was reasonably active in district affairs and half-heartedly ran for district trustee for the UUA board but was defeated. I had not been involved in nor did I participate in continental denominational affairs except for supporting the Annual Program Fund and attending most General Assemblies. When I was still very new in Richmond, I preached a sermon threatening to resign if the church didn't make its annual fund goal. I never did that again. But not until I came to 25 and saw the larger picture did I fully appreciate that, while Atlanta was becoming a large church, a number of the large churches in the Association were becoming small churches.

"I still think of Atlanta as the high point of my ministerial career. It was there that I proved myself. Those were exciting, growing, and difficult years. I was never able to change my leadership style from that which was appropriate to a small congregation to that which was appropriate to a large one. However, over time I changed personally, becoming less compulsive and controlling in my behavior. I decided I wanted a change. I needed a situation that had less pressure and fewer demands on me personally.

"I arrived at 25 in a state of relative innocence concerning both what it would be like to work at headquarters and the state of the Association.

"For me, personally, it was a very pleasant change. I enjoyed working from nine to five, no telephone calls during the dinner hour, and reading for pleasure instead of for sermon ideas. I even enjoyed the daily commute by train from Needham into Boston.

"The mood of the Association was something else. Throughout much of the Association the mood was pessimistic, distrustful, and discouraged. There had been a great deal of divisiveness over various issues: black empowerment, gay and lesbian concerns, feminism, district structure, etc. Our membership had been declining for a number of years. Relations between the administration and the board of trustees had deteriorated and were increasingly more adversarial. Traveling staff members would return from field trips exhausted and demoralized. At headquarters, budgets were being cut, staff reduced, and programs and services curtailed.

"When Bob West became president, he found that the UUA had incurred a sizable debt, Beacon Press was requiring ever-increasing subsidies, and financial support from the churches was not keeping up with inflation. Bob West was president during one of the most difficult periods in the life of the Association. He had to overcome tremendous obstacles to keep the Association solvent while keeping it operating—and it operated at a surprising degree of effectiveness. He stabilized the finances of the Association and instituted personnel policies and procedures, which brought order and fairness to the headquarters operation. He established a good working relationship with the Veatch Program and the North Shore Unitarian Universalist Congregation in Plandome. This helped the Association to come through its financial crises. He initiated court action to break the Holdeen Trust, which did not bear fruit until my administration. He laid the groundwork for making the IARF a viable international religious organization. . . .

"Bob was a strong, competent administrator and exceedingly conscientious about being on top of every detail of the operation. By the time I arrived at 25, he seemed to me to be worn down, experiencing minimal enjoyment or satisfaction from the job. It was my impression that he was feeling very much alone—unsupported and unappreciated. I was personally fond of him and tried to be supportive and encouraging, both on the job and off. Our relationship was strong enough that I could differ with him and offer what I thought was constructive criticism. It seemed to me he was much more defensive than he needed to be. He did not seek advice readily and took few into his confidence. I know he was deeply hurt by his experience at 25. His office door was usually closed—a telling symbol of his aloneness. Being president had taken a heavy personal toll.

"In 1975, because of further budget cuts, Bob West instituted a staff reorganization. The Departments of Ministry, Extension, Inter-District Program, Education, and Social Responsibility were combined into one Department of Ministerial and Congregational Services, and I was asked to become the director. The reorganization caused a major disruption at 25 and created a great deal of controversy among the professional leaders, in the districts, and in the churches. I was dispatched to ministers' meetings and district meetings to explain and justify the reorganization. This was the first time I had come face to face with an angry and hostile constituency. I thought there must be a better way of bringing about change, and it crossed my mind that there must be a better way of making a living. I had more success with district and lay leaders than I did with our professional leaders (I was almost thrown out of a ministers' meeting in Maine). This proved to be the beginning of a good and positive relationship with district and lay leaders that became influential several years later in my becoming president.

"With the election of a new President in 1977, my future at 25 was uncertain, especially since I was a member of the executive staff. It is not unreasonable to think that a new president would want his or her own cabinet. I did not know any of the three candidates well, Paul least of all. So I was preparing myself psychologically to move on.

"When Paul arrived at 25 in the summer of 1977, he asked all of the executive staff to stay on. He had in mind no immediate or major changes in programs or structure. . . . Paul's health began deteriorating, and more and more of the decision-making and program-planning fell to Bob Senghas and to me. As Paul began to talk about not running for a second term, I began to think seriously about running myself—with a great deal of encouragement from Bill Schulz. I discussed the idea with the interdistrict representatives to get a reading on potential support from district leaders. Their response was positive. I had also received encouragement from Ken MacLean and Mary Hart, who were serving on the UUA board of trustees. But there was no 'Draft Pickett' movement building, and many of my colleagues were hoping for a charismatic leader to emerge."

Years later, as his own presidency was coming to an end, Pickett commented, "I have never lost sight of the fact that I was appointed by the board of trustees to this position by the slimmest of margins. And I probably would never have been elected president if I had run in a contested election campaign. I disliked even the limited amount of politicking required to procure the necessary votes from among the twenty-six members of the board!"

Gene received a strong vote of support from a list of ninety-four clergy and laypersons from across the continent, who voiced their endorsement with these words in a letter on April 18, 1979: "We, the undersigned, urge the board of trustees of the UUA to appoint Eugene Pickett as president of our Association to fill out the unexpired term left by the death of Paul Carnes. For the past five years Gene Pickett has served the UUA in positions of leadership and responsibility. He has played a major role in many of the programs which have been developed in that time. He has displayed imagination, flexibility, and a capacity to work creatively with others. He is a superb administrator and is totally familiar with the organization of our Association. . . . We do not believe that we can afford to mark time for two years with an interim president. There are many constructive things happening in our movement; to continue their momentum and gather new support and participants, we need the sort of vigorous leadership Gene Pickett can provide."

Gordon McKeeman, who had just completed his term on the board of trustees, sought the post at the urging of some board members who felt it was time to have a minister of Universalist heritage at the helm of the UUA. Others felt the presidency should go to Jack Mendelsohn who was the close runner-up in the three-way race among Carnes, McKeeman, and Mendelsohn in 1975, but Jack was throwing his support to Gene. When the April meeting drew near, the board was about evenly split between Pickett and McKeeman. Sandra Caron, moderator on the board, held the vote to break a tie. She supported Gene.

Board members Nathaniel Lauriat and William Donovan voted for themselves on the first ballot, with Pickett receiving thirteen votes and McKeeman garnering eleven. The second and final vote was fourteen to twelve. Barely escaping a thirteen to thirteen tie, Gene Pickett was elected to the presidency of the UUA by a majority of one vote. Gene recalls the moment as being fraught with terror: "Upon hearing the vote, I grew really scared, and in those kinds of situations my anxiety runs wild. I bumbled through, picking up the concession instead of the victory speech. My other feeling was that Bill [Schulz] wasn't anywhere to be seen. I was still very dependent upon him. He and his wife Linda Lu had gone to Florida to visit his Aunt Dolly. I thought to myself, 'I just don't believe this, his having been so supportive, and then not being there with me at the moment of decision.' Helen was at work, so she wasn't present either. There I was, standing alone, without either my wife or buddy to support me. I felt abandoned in my big moment."

Opposition to Gene among the board members afforded inconsequential backlash to his election. Even those who voted out of loyalty to Gordon personally liked and respected Gene. So the board morale, despite a closely divided vote, remained strong.

The Pickett Years, 1979-1985

On the strength of a winter spirit, spring began.
Where before scarcity ruled, hard effort came
to nothing, discouragement prevailed.
Now came yes bursting through uncertainty,
insisting, finding a way:
the door open,
the words quiet, hopeful,
the faith clear,
the spirit strong, contagious,
engendering growth.

FOR GENE PICKETT FROM JOAN GOODWIN

New Faces

On becoming president in 1979, Pickett made three major staff appointments. The Reverend Joyce H. Smith was named to succeed him as director of the Department of Ministerial and Congregational Services. Dr. Robert C. Sallies was appointed treasurer and financial vice president to replace Arthur Root, who was soon to retire. Dr. William F. Schulz was named executive vice president. Dr. Robert E. Senghas had indicated his desire to return to the parish ministry, and for Pickett, Bill was the obvious choice, for he had become a trusted advisor and personal friend and was familiar with the administration and organization at 25 Beacon Street.

Pickett's first challenge was to forge a better working relationship with the UUA board of trustees. The interaction had deteriorated during previous administrations. A major complaint was that the administration screened background information, only letting the board in on the closing decisions. Immediately, the Pickett administration was fully forthcoming, supplying the board with all relevant material. Pickett's mode of collaboration was both natural and politically smart. He considered himself a steward, not an owner, of the Association during his tenure as president.

"On becoming president I knew fairly well what I was getting into," Pickett wrote. "Unlike previous presidents, I knew in considerable detail and depth the financial situation, the operation of headquarters, and the tenor of the board of trustees. Also, I had a good reading on the dissatisfactions and expectations of our churches and fellowships.

"In addition, I knew my own strengths and limitations. I had always enjoyed the pastoral and organizational aspects of the ministry. I was experienced and successful in these areas. I related well to people and enjoyed working with them.

"I was a strong institutionalist and knew well that the values and ideals of liberal religion could be effective and influential only if they had a vital and solid institutional base. But I also knew that we as a religious movement have traditionally been suspicious of a strong centralized Association. We have been fearful that strength would mean power, rigidity, and control. But I am convinced that our Association can be both strong *and* flexible—an institution of which one can be critical while still being committed to it.

"The Association has become the whipping boy for many of our discontents and dissatisfactions. We are fearful that it will attempt to put us into boxes. I think we professional leaders have a strong propensity for putting *ourselves* into boxes—seeing situations in terms of either/or rather than both/and. Power in our Association does not lie in being able to force people into boxes. Rather, it lies in balancing our varying needs, in honoring our diverse feelings, in reconciling our differences. I believe this honoring of diversity was one of my major strengths as parish minister and as president.

"When I became president, the Association had gone through almost a decade of budget cuts and staff reductions. Many of our programs and services were in danger of becoming little more than holding actions. Religious education needed evaluation and a new direction. LRY [Liberal Religious Youth] had become almost nonexistent. There was a great deal of dissatisfaction with the resolutions process. The Department of Ministry was understaffed, and the relationship with the theological schools needed attention. The district program was inadequately staffed to deliver programs and services effectively. Beacon Press was floundering. There were limited funds for extension, and we had no well-defined strategy for growth. Our fund-raising efforts had to be reconstituted. There were indeed a great many institutional repairs to be made and much building to be done.

"While I knew my areas of competency, I was also aware of my limitations. I am much more a private person than a public one. This was always a source of anxiety, both in the parish and the presidency. I couldn't offer a prayer in public without my note cards. Public confrontation, be it picket lines or protest marches, always caused sleepless nights and an unsettled stomach. A lack of self-confidence made me uncomfortable with the rich and famous—not that this problem arose very often (either in the parish *or* in the presidency), but it did make fund-raising more difficult. I always thought of myself as a populist president, yet I held the *office* of president in high regard, and was always sensitive to slights and disrespect for the office. I had a strong sense of oughtness and a real appreciation for the importance of the public aspect of the residency, and so I tried. It was not easy and not always effective, and the constant pressure took its toll. . . .

"Another of my first orders of business was to improve the relationship between the Administration and the board of trustees. This relationship had become increasingly adversarial. For example, the budgeting process would consume days in argumentation and, frequently, hostility. We in the administration began by being more open in sharing information and outlining our plans. We developed closer working relationships with individual trustees. While some disagreements remained, we moved quickly to a greater degree of cooperation and trust.

"For several years the board, at its retreats, had worked at defining the role of the board in relation to the moderator, the president, and the administration. The issue was never fully resolved, and so there remained differences in expectations and ambiguity about board responsibilities. I saw the board's duties as being primarily to make policy, to review program plans and budget, to evaluate the effectiveness of the organization and the administration, to represent the needs and interests of their constituencies, and to represent the Association to their constituencies. In my view, the administration and staff should have primary responsibility for the development and implementation of programs and services. But there were differences of opinion on this matter—some members feeling that the board should be more involved in program-planning and development. This was an area where I felt the moderator and I differed in significant measure. While my differences with her did not affect my overall relationship with the board, they were a source of tension and stress for me. Though Sandy had supported my being appointed president and did support most of my initiatives, our personal relationship deteriorated over the six years, and this, for me, was one of the most difficult and unfortunate aspects of my presidency."

Moderator Sandra Caron was supportive of Pickett's appointment as president, and their working relationship began well. Conflicts between Pickett and Caron would surface later when she desired a version of shared presidency that was not to materialize. Nevertheless, the role and responsibilities of moderator were expanded during her term of office. When Joseph Fisher had been moderator (1964-1977), he primarily chaired the board and General Assembly and consulted with the president. With Pickett's support, Caron traveled extensively to represent the UUA at formal public functions, dividing these duties with the president.

Their personalities gradually clashed and sabotaged the level of teamwork either would have desired. To their credit,

Pickett and Caron's personal conflicts never contaminated the board process. As an institutionalist, Pickett refused to let their interpersonal squabbles injure the overall Association. However, there can be little doubt that both of them suffered personally.

Pickett believes that the present system of UUA governance remains flexible enough and works well for a collaborative style of leadership. He contends that no system will prove effective if you do not have the right people in place. He supports the continuation of the current power balance between the board and the administration and opposed the 1994 proposal of the Commission on Governance, which would have changed the nature of the presidency and recommended that the selection of a chief executive officer be made by the UUA board of trustees.

Pickett wrote in the March/April 1994 *World*: "Sound management depends principally on building good collaborative relationships with people and establishing clear responsibilities and lines of communication. Effective administrators choose staff who complement their strengths and weaknesses, and the current system allows very well for this."

There were times during his tenure as president when Gene found it best to say, "I'm sorry, I made a mistake," even when others equally culpable failed to do so. Temperamentally, he was never one to lash out at others but rather one to internalize the frustrations and criticisms.

Despite being hurt and disappointed periodically during his presidency, Gene never lapsed into despair. He still encountered episodes of mild depression, but he was never trapped in the deep melancholy he felt at Meadville and Atlanta. Staff firings, and there were a few, were tough for Gene, who is a conciliator by personality and conviction. He would try to negotiate matters peaceably, but occasionally the difficulties became insurmountable. There were other aspects of the presidency that were troublesome for Gene, especially the public functions, but there was nothing that overwhelmed him.

Again, the friendship of Bill Schulz played a crucial role. After Helen, Bill was Gene's closest advisor. Another person who became important in the final years of Gene's administration was Kathleen (Kay) Montgomery, who joined the Development Department staff in 1983 during Gene's second term. Kay had been very active in the Atlanta church, chairing the adult education program while Gene was minister. Later she was president of the Mid-South District and served on several continental committees. Her experience with local congregations and in the district equipped her to make valuable contributions at the headquarters level, and she became a close friend of Gene's.

The Imposter Syndrome

Speechmaking, although not as pressurized a situation as weekly sermons in the parish, still presented a challenge for Gene. He was beset by anxiety attacks whenever he knew a talk was required. He also never felt at ease making impromptu prayers or spontaneous responses at public gatherings, and would rely on prepared notes to guide him. Many of his speeches were collaboratively shaped with substantive support from both Helen and Bill Schulz. Helen would modify Bill's suggestions to make sure the resultant talk sounded like Gene. Pickett tried various other speech writers but none of them were effective.

On one occasion, Gene was traveling to Washington, DC, to speak against apartheid in South Africa. Pickett's speech writer at the time had prepared a statement that Gene did not study until moments before he arrived. Riding on the bus, he glanced at the speech, then froze with panic: "My God, I can't say this! These are neither my sentiments nor my words!" He rapidly reworked the talk as best he could just in time for his delivery.

Gene was apprehensive of public appearances of any sort, including television and radio. He did well with a question and answer format focusing on denominational programs, but he felt that he floundered when addressing abstract theological or political issues.

In addition, Gene never enjoyed greeting celebrated people, whether in secular or religious circles. His impostor syndrome would rear its ugly head, and he felt intimidated by them. Gene did not actually mind meeting these individuals, but encountering them in his role as president was a problem. It was contrary to his character to trade on his position. Pickett knew it would have been a substantial asset if he had been able to represent the UUA confidently in the public realm, but he simply couldn't project himself as anybody important.

Reluctant Yet Ready Leader

Despite his anxieties, Pickett had risen to leadership positions throughout his life. He was class president in high school and in his seminary career at Meadville. He was always willing, even with persistent feelings of inadequacy, to serve at the helm of any group he joined. Pickett was unquestionably one of the most capable presidents in our twentieth-century denominational history in terms of relational support, organizational vitality, and programmatic accomplishment. His own description of the many roles the president was called upon to fill serves to illuminate the difficulties inherent in meeting the expectations:

"The role of president of our Association is complex and ambiguous. The president serves as religious leader (which includes an important ceremonial role), as the public and at times prophetic spokesperson for the movement, as pastor-at-large, and as the chief executive officer of a small bureaucracy. There frequently is confusion in role expectations. It is all but impossible to fulfill the mixed expectations and respond to the varied demands. To complicate the picture, I found that many colleagues have difficulty in relating to those in leadership positions. Many of us like to keep our leaders in their place and can be quick with a put-down. This can be quite effective in making a person feel inadequate—especially if one already has self-doubts. To be accepted and respected by my colleagues was very important to me, and so perhaps I was over-sensitive to . . . expressions of disapproval. While president, I was seldom invited to ministerial gatherings. If I was invited, it usually was to be put on the hot-seat. As ministers and leaders we need, I think, to look seriously at how to develop greater trust, mutuality, and understanding among all levels of leadership.

"While much of my effort was directed toward institution-building, I was well aware that the concern for programs and services, growth, and financial stability would be for naught unless we did better at speaking to the quality of our religious experience and to the depth dimension of our faith. We needed to be about the task of reconstituting a Unitarian Universalism of substance and inspiration. It was with this concern in mind that we initiated at General Assemblies the President's Colloquium on Theology. The time seemed to be right, for many of our members were expressing genuine interest in the theological dimensions of our faith.

"I was not well suited to provide leadership for this task. I had always found it difficult to articulate clearly and compellingly the faith that had motivated and sustained me. But I identified with and was somewhat comforted by Whitehead's description of depth as the 'power to take into account all those factors in a situation which can*not* be adequately articulated.'

"What theological insights I have articulated have generally been gained in the context of very personal experiences. Those experiences—which have been nurturing and renewing, revealing and affirming—have been most intense at times of loneliness, pain, and uncertainty. I described my 'wintry spirituality' in one of my General Assembly reports. This description elicited more reaction, both of concern and appreciation, than perhaps any other remarks I made while I was president. My search for a sustaining faith—or a means to salvation, if you will—as a teenager, during theological school, and in the ministry, took many directions. But it was in grappling with uncertainty and ambiguity, with pain and loneliness and the mystery of death that I was to discover meaning and hope.

"On thinking back on my motivation for entering the Unitarian Universalist ministry, I realize now that it, too, was part of my search for a means to salvation. By that time, I was convinced that if I was to be saved, it would be by way of good works and not by grace. I have spent my life as a minister striving to do good works. I find it ironical that I may yet be saved—by grace. For I have been reflecting on Tillich's description of grace. He says, 'Sometimes a wave of light breaks into our darkness, and it is as though a voice were saying, 'You are accepted, accepted by that which is greater than you, and the name of which you do not know.' If that happens to us, we experience grace.' Now it occurs to me that if salvation comes, it probably will be as a small wave of light borne into my darkness on a wintry wind."

The paradoxical tension that has driven Gene Pickett is expressed in one of his favorite quotations in W. H. Auden's incisive introduction to Dag Hammarskjold's classic book, *Markings*: "To be gifted but not to know how best to make use of one's gifts, to be highly ambitious but at the same time to feel unworthy, is a dangerous combination which can often end in mental breakdown or suicide and, as the earlier entries show, the thought of suicide was not strange to Hammarskjold."

An illustrious Hammarskjold affirmation captures Pickett's pilgrimage as well: "In a dream I walked with God through the deep places of creation, past walls that receded and gates that opened . . . until around me was an infinity into which we all flowed together, and lived anew, like the rings made by raindrops, falling upon wide expanses of calm waters. I don't know who or what put the question, I don't know when it was put . . . I don't even remember answering. But at some moment I did answer Yes to someone or something and from that hour I was certain that existence is meaningful."

Despite his gnawing insecurities and self-doubts, Pickett rarely hesitated to stride forward, to say yes to life's grand summons. He neither shirked responsibilities nor avoided troubles. Yet as he would amend Hammarskjold: "I never exactly knew who or what I was saying yes to!"

If there was one major figure in the sweep of contemporary history who most shaped Pickett's philosophy of life, it is Dag Hammarskjold. Gene acknowledges his indebtedness in a sermon given in Atlanta: "Reading Hammarskjold's book *Markings*, published after his death, had a major influence on my thinking. His appealing mysticism modified and softened the rough edges of the humanism which undergirded my belief system. He was a committed person of faith who both shunned and was attracted to power, who heard the call of the spirit as clearly as he heard the voices of the world. He was essentially a poet of ambiguity and loneliness. And this, I know, had great appeal for me. But his work and writing have been a witness and testimony to hope. Out of the uncertainties and loneliness of my own life I have discovered a basis for hope in Hammarskjold which has given meaning to my own existence and created a sustaining vitality for my religious faith."

In the same sermon, Pickett elaborates upon his life-affirming outlook: "Each of us has the power, and, therefore, the responsibility to give ourselves to what matters: truth and decency, love and justice. Each of us has the power, and therefore, the obligation to give ourselves to life . . . to say Yes to life. And so, the basis for our hope is both possibility and commitment.

"We must choose, despite the ambiguity, uncertainty and loneliness of life. Our choices determine the quality and meaning of our lives. While hope never says that the outcome is sure, it does say that the possibility and the commitment are worth the venture. The story of humankind is the story of disappointed hopes slowly transformed into hopes fulfilled."

One is equally reminded of Ralph Waldo Emerson's suggestive phrase: "God has need of a person here!" Gene was the kind of person Emerson had in mind: he was fully himself, without duplicity or mask. Pickett was essentially the same person privately and publicly—a rare feat for political figures. A leader with such genuineness and integrity was precisely the person the Association needed to govern during this epoch of history.

Traveling the Halls and Hills

Gene Pickett served as a pastoral minister to the staff. People came to work at 25 Beacon Street envisioning that it would resemble a unified, cozy congregation, but since staff members did not live, and rarely socialized, together, their expectations for intimate community were often disappointed. But during work hours, Gene was mindful of everyone. He spent time traveling the halls, moving among staff cohorts on errands of business and kindness. Gene knew what staff members were doing and was generous with his appreciation.

Although Gene as president was charged with a greater range of responsibilities than he had assumed in the parish, he didn't feel the burning need to control everything. He couldn't. As president he started with a cooperative staff and bureaucracy already in place. He surrounded himself with high-powered leaders in their own right who willingly collaborated with him, persons who were strong and compassionately critical. He had never benefited from the depth or breadth of such co-workers in his parish ministries.

In the Atlanta church Gene had felt overwhelmed by the thousand or more persons he felt obligated to engage personally in the congregational context. At the UUA, the lines of accountability were clearly drawn and equitably shared. He could maintain a personal and caring approach with the more than 100 staff members at headquarters and be effective without being compulsive. As Max De Pree says in *Leadership Jazz*: "at the core of becoming a leader is the need always to connect one's voice with one's touch." Gene was able to connect his voice and touch at the UUA in a mutually satisfying fashion.

Pickett's door was invariably open. He was a visible leader. He was a caregiver not a caretaker, establishing direct communication yet maintaining essential boundaries. When there was a personal concern, he was suitably responsive. Once when a staff member was struggling with an alcohol problem, Gene said, "We'll pay to send you for treatment if you're willing, and you can have your job back if the treatment is successful." The staff member was successful in recovery and remains profusely grateful to Gene.

Another long-time staff member, Eugene Navias, shared

the following story in the July/August 1994 issue of the *World*: "When I applied for the job of director of the Religious Education Department, more than ten years had gone by since the first GA resolutions, and still I worried that the UUA would not appoint an openly gay man to a sensitive post involving the religious education of children and youth. So I went to Gene Pickett, then UUA president, to face the question before the day of my interview.

"'As you probably know,' I said to Gene, 'I am gay, and I'm wondering whether that will make any difference in my candidacy for the job.'

"'You know,' Gene responded, 'you've never told me directly that you're gay, even though others have told me you've come out. What response have you had from people around the denomination?'

"'I've had nothing but positive responses. People have thanked me for sharing with them. It just hasn't seemed to make any difference.'

"'Well,' he said, 'that's the way I feel. I'm glad you told me yourself, and I can assure you it does not make any difference.'

"I was so choked up, grateful, relieved that I just mumbled some incoherent thanks and left. Bless Gene Pickett. I know of no other religious denomination in this society where that could have happened in 1982.

"Finally out of the closet, I could put the divided parts of my life together. I found I could love and enter a committed relationship with a partner, which has now lasted some twelve years."

Pickett traveled the hills of the continent as well as the

halls of 25 Beacon Street. He listened long and hard to the views of Unitarian Universalists—North and South, East and West. He was more comfortable circulating among the laity, because "I never felt fully accepted or respected by my colleagues, especially after I joined the headquarters staff."

Pickett was wounded on more than one occasion by the snide barbs of clergy colleagues who considered him fair game as the administrative pilot of the Unitarian Universalist movement. UUA presidents have used different tactics to withstand "the icy, abrasive blasts from the field." Greeley possessed the knack of selective listening. Schulz would often retaliate. Pickett would absorb the punishment while trying to hold his ground.

Altogether, the presidency enabled Gene to use most of his gifts—organizational, interpersonal, and programmatic—without being engulfed by the all-consuming strains of parish ministry. But since he, as well as his marriage, were in far better emotional shape when he arrived in Boston, it is hard to predict what would have happened if Gene had remained in the parish. After his six plus years in office, would he have run again for president if there had been no term limit?

"No, I think I wanted to quit while things were going well and I was feeling good," says Pickett. "Now, Dana said he would stay forever! He was unflappable and unfazed by it all, but I wanted to make sure I got out intact."

Few presidents in the history of either Unitarianism or Universalism have gone through their full terms feeling extremely positive. Gene did not want to push his luck any further. Some supporters tried to have the bylaws changed to dispense with the term limit so that Gene could run again, but he was firm in his resolve to leave the presidency at the end of his second term. In fact, Pickett concluded all of his professional positions precisely when things were still going well.

Pickett House

When traveling as the UUA's representative, Gene would often stay at modest hotels, feeling it would be elitist to use the local equivalent of the Ritz. He appreciated the good life, but as president he felt it was wrong to pull rank or to benefit from special privilege. As Helen noted, "Gene was uncomfortable with the trappings of rank that accompany the presidency, few though they were! And during his years in the parish ministry, he was never even able to bring himself to reserve a minister's parking space at the church. This was more of a problem for me than for Gene, for on occasion I would arrive a little late for the second service with three young children in tow and have to park well down the road." Gene felt more comfortable being perceived as a leader among, rather than apart from, the people. The naming of an entire building after him, is a case in point.

Pickett House and Eliot House are UUA guest houses with meeting rooms located at 6 and 7 Mount Vernon Place in Boston, about one block from 25 Beacon Street. Eliot House, acquired in 1959, is named for American Unitarian Association president Frederick May Eliot and was used for many years as office space. Pickett House was acquired in 1981 to provide lodging for UUA board and committee meetings. The two building were joined together and beautifully restored in the late 1980s.

At Gene's final board meeting as president, the members presented Gene with a beautiful plaque which they then attached to the Pickett House. The rationale was that he had been an outstanding president and that the house had been purchased during his term of office. Yet, true to his character, Gene thought it set a bad precedent, because there would never be enough structures to name after all future or past presidents. Nonetheless, the board profoundly appreciated Pickett and wanted to do something special in his honor, so they named a building for an improbable president, who would never have even allowed one of the restrooms to be named for himself if it had been his decision to make.

Before Bill Schulz became president he would say, "You are loved, Gene. I will be respected, but I wish I could be loved." In truth, Gene Pickett was generally both loved *and* respected as president. Bill elaborated upon his deep bond with Gene in the summation essay of his own presidency in the May/June 1993 issue of the *World*: "For no one with whom I have worked at the UUA over the past fifteen years do I have more respect and affection than I have for Gene Pickett. That is not because he appointed me executive vice president; indeed, we clashed sharply more than once in our six years working together. But Gene Pickett has a largesse of soul, a generosity of spirit and yet a distinctly modest mien that I have always admired deeply. On top of that he is institutionally imaginative and politically astute. Because he is not flashy, he has rarely been given adequate credit for his productive years as president."

Gene felt strongly about his friendship with Bill as well and earlier had introduced his successor to the presidency with these sentiments: "If I had hand-picked my successor, I could not have made a better selection. Bill Schulz is a creative, competent, and confident leader; he is thoughtful and provocative, young and energetic. Indeed, his youth was an issue in the election, but people need not have worried. The job ages one quickly.

"Bill has been a close and dear friend as well as a most valued advisor. He hasn't always been the easiest person to get along with, but he could add excitement to even the tedious task of budget preparation and helped overall to make the job of being president fun. And that is a rare talent. I have never enjoyed working with anyone as much as with Bill, and together we made significant achievements in extending and strengthening our movement. I would like to have had a son like Bill!"

In a different vein, Bill made the following remarks at Gene's retirement party: "Now I count Gene as beloved a friend as I have, but Helen will know what I mean when I say sometimes he can be positively exasperating. Part of Gene's script in life is to be dissatisfied—mostly with himself but also with those of us who love him. If we love him too little, he, of course, becomes dejected. If we love him too much, he becomes suspicious. 'I'm not worthy of all that love,' he thinks to himself. 'They must be putting me on.' Imagine how confused Gene will be at the end of this evening's celebration.

"Fortunately, one of the most appealing things about Gene is that he is profoundly aware of how neurotic he is. Indeed, I believe him to be capable of greater authenticity— by which I mean non-manipulative self-disclosure—than almost any man I know."

As a collaborator, Pickett felt unthreatened by former UUA presidents. In fact, he wanted them by his side and he plumbed their wisdom. West was not interested in returning, but Dana Greeley felt honored and thrilled to be invited back. Gene was initially in awe of Greeley, but as time wore on, he felt privileged to have Greeley's resources. Gene also welcomed his Universalist predecessors Robert Cummins and Philip Giles. Gene didn't need to dominate his own show. He chose to share the limelight, the glory, the mission. In limerick verse, his long and trusted associate, Joyce Smith, captured Pickett's gift:

> A UUA President called Gene
> Was famous for building a team
> He blended the best
> And put them to test
> And showed what our religion could mean.
> There was a fine president named Pickett
> Who made a fair garden of a thicket
> With care and Veatch bucks
> And a modest "Oh shucks"
> When faced with a problem he'd lick it.

An Activist President

Pickett was described by Bill Schulz as an "activist President." Gene was indeed an energetic, active force in the sense of being intimately involved with the development of programs and services and with the administration of the UUA. He frequently called and checked with both staff and board, staying up-to-date on all programmatic and political matters. It was not his forte, however, to be an activist in the style of Dana Greeley, leading a civil rights march with Martin Luther King, Jr., across the bridge in Selma, Alabama. He was an administrative force rather than a prophetic presence.

In 1987, as he was laboring feverishly on what was to be the major address of his career, the Berry Street Essay, Pickett surprised himself by the list he compiled of solid accomplishments of his presidency. In fact, so many goals had been reached that Bill Schulz bemoaned that it left him relatively little to initiate during his tenure.

Gene was quick to point out that the Association had gone through a period of budget cuts and staff reductions before he assumed office, so there was a hunger to get programs rolling. It was Pickett who set things into motion, igniting people and generating programmatic excitement and outcome. He was a leader who combined imagination and activism. He brought the best out in people, served goals, and produced results larger than his own identity. He was an authority in the fullest sense of a word that comes from the Latin verb *augere,* meaning to cause to grow, to augment that which already is. As a leader Pickett enhanced the gifts of those around him.

When described as a practical rather than a philosophical theologian, Gene would concur with the practical part but would refrain from even claiming the label theologian. He sums up his approach as follows: "I am more comfortable with the idea of being a pragmatist or living one's faith and values than I am with being a theologian. I have always grounded my ministry more in the insights of psychology and social science than theology. For me, the key question of the religious journey is how do you lead a principled life. Our mission is to be meaning-makers."

When Pickett was asked to describe his leadership style with rapid-fire adjectives, his understandable response drew a smile: "I'm not a spontaneous kind of leader, but I can prepare to be spontaneous by tomorrow!" The strongest statement Pickett musters with respect to his leadership is his perennial proviso that he was simply fortunate to be in the right place at the right time, be it his southern ministries in Miami, Richmond, and Atlanta, or his transition to the UUA presidency. He deems them good matches born of providential coincidence and downplays his bountiful gifts and skills.

In Gene's entire life, the only situation in which he was passive or reactive was during his childhood in an entangled relationship with a domineering mother. Even there, his resoluteness for change drove him to risk therapy and sustain a remarkable transformation. He was never merely the right person at the right time, as he contends. Things did not merely happen to Gene Pickett; he consistently made things happen. One is reminded of the Robert Frost phrase: "How hard it is to keep from being king when it's in you and in the situation. . . ." Henry Ford put it more bluntly: "The question, 'who ought to be boss?' is like asking 'who ought to be the tenor in the quartet?'. Obviously, the person who can sing tenor!"

Shakespeare wrote that "some are born great . . . others have greatness thrust upon them." In the case of Gene Pickett, he evolved into greatness, and as one would anticipate, Gene is comfortable with the term "evolve" but not the label of "greatness." What drove Pickett to be a consummate molder of people? It was partly his survival instinct and burning desire to establish a sense of adequacy during his professional life. He was also plentifully equipped with an array of essential, though often underrated, qualities of character like perseverance, organizational savvy, flexibility in the midst of dissent, and natural kindness toward people.

Pickett was also not so ego-focused that he could not be open to critique or suggestion. If someone offered an idea that Gene thought was superior to the one he currently espoused, he would say, "Let's go with yours!" He was not wed to tradition or personal agenda; he kept his eyes on a vision that surpassed the immediate or the familiar. Thus he encouraged new possibilities and divergent views. For example, he brought in the district presidents to set priorities for their own programs in the face of budget cuts, so that when the board made tough decisions, they were more universally accepted in the field.

Although Pickett excelled in conflict negotiations, he would also ferry unresolved tension home. In his valiant efforts to generate win-win situations for all parties involved, his calm exterior belied a wildly churning stomach. He would offer direct criticism when warranted, yet he was not one to scold or disparage his associates or opponents. Furthermore, different factions always knew Pickett would treat them fairly and serve them equally. Gene was a dogged leader, but because he was flexible in listening to others, and willing to change his views, he was often misjudged to be a pushover. Hardly. He possessed moral backbone and mental steeliness.

His most difficult presidential duty, apart from public presentations, was confronting people in anger. Although he would not sidestep contention, expressing anger was his short suit at home and at work: "I don't get genuinely mad at someone with a good, healthy anger." In the early years of their marriage, Gene would freeze Helen out when he was angry, not talking to her for days. Therapy revealed that Gene had been sitting on a volcano of fury that he vented against himself through states of depression. In his later years, although he still did not view anger as positive, Gene was able to dissipate rage more frequently through his growing assertiveness.

Overall, Pickett thoroughly enjoyed the presidency, and the post evinced his best qualities and capitalized upon his competencies despite the fierce trepidation he experienced whenever he had to perform publicly. He enjoyed working with the staff to develop programs, visiting districts to explain the UUA, and representing Unitarian Universalism through his international travels. His relationship with Helen was clearly reinvigorated during this period. In summary, he reflected, "I got enough rewards and positive feedback to far outweigh the negative."

A Shared Presidency

Although Gene's first term was definite for only two years, the Picketts decided to gamble and move into the president's residence, knowing that they conceivably would have to move out again. A huge, six-story row house at the foot of Beacon Hill, 33 Brimmer Street was essentially unfurnished and had no elevator. It took Helen an entire year to finish settling in with curtains on all the windows and towels in all the bathrooms. The UUA board and committees were entertained regularly at the Pickett home, events that proved physically taxing for Helen yet immensely gratifying for Unitarian Universalist staff and leaders throughout the denomination.

Because Gene was able to come home for dinner at 5:00 P.M. many evenings, especially during their first years in Boston, the Picketts were finally able to enjoy some social time alone. They even bought season tickets to the open rehearsals of the Boston Symphony Orchestra. As president, Gene traveled about five out of six weekends, so during the week he scrambled to catch up on work from the office, thus curtailing their leisure time significantly. But the time they spent together during Gene's presidency was a major advance over the relational malnutrition of parish life, because they were together most of those weekend trips.

Helen no longer felt deprived. By the second year she had quit her job at Wellesley and was traveling with Gene almost everywhere he went, primarily because he traveled over sixty percent of the time and they didn't want to be separated that much, and secondly, because they found that Helen served as "an informal staff aide, who could observe and evaluate, sympathize and commiserate, and help keep Gene organized." As Gene recalls, "Helen traveled extensively with me and was an excellent representative for the Association. In many respects it was a shared presidency."

Helen remembers some trips as grueling and difficult, but most were interesting and exciting adventures: visiting churches around the United States and Canada; sojourning to the British Unitarian General Assembly and the Unitarian churches in Hungary and Transylvania, and trekking to

India and Japan. She remarks, "The whole experience of the presidency was one we never expected to have, never dreamed of having, and it was a privilege for which we are profoundly grateful."

Helen continued to share in the writing aspect of the presidency, scouring Gene's reports and speeches before he delivered them. She attended most of the board meetings as an observer who furnished Gene with an additional set of ears and eyes. Helen felt integrally involved and proved of enormous assistance to him both intellectually and emotionally. The fact that she had attended seminary was an asset that helped her speak articulately when questions were posed about the religious and ethical issues involved.

In the portrait of Gene Pickett painted at the close of his second term and hanging at 25 Beacon Street, a photograph of Helen rests near Gene's right elbow, emphasizing her vital presence as his devoted helpmate. Theirs was singularly a partnered presidency.

Helen recalls the unveiling of Gene's painting: "Toward the end of his term, Gene chose an artist to paint his portrait. I was very eager to see it, and to see whether Gene's likeness had been captured to my satisfaction. The unveiling took place at an all-staff farewell party, and I studied the painting for several moments before I saw that I had been included in the portrait. As a surprise for me, Gene had asked the artist to include a miniature portrait of me. I can think of no lovelier tribute than for Gene to have shared his portrait with me. A person who is still essentially private and not easily verbal found a way to speak volumes!"

The State of the Union

"I believe that the first test of a truly great person is their humility. I do not mean, by humility, doubt of their own power. But really great individuals have a curious feeling that the greatness is not in them, but through them. And they see something divine in every other person and are endlessly, foolishly, incredibly merciful."

JOHN RUSKIN

1979—East Lansing

Although speechmaking was always a gut-wrenching ordeal for Gene, when his seven "state of the union" addresses at the General Assemblies from 1979 through 1985 are reviewed, one is moved by the powerful blend of practical achievement and philosophical inspiration. Gene will never be remembered as a charismatic speaker, but his speeches reveal telling insights about this essentially private, improbable president. Hearing Gene speak, one is struck not by his rhetoric so much as by his genuineness. He is a practitioner of lucid communication rather than elegant delivery. He conveys depth without pedantry or pretentiousness.

In his inaugural address as president in 1979 in East Lansing, Michigan, he began engagingly with typical poignancy, dry wit, and sufficient, but understated, ego: "I stand here today acutely aware of my own limitations but possessed of the most abiding faith in our movement and its future. I stand here somewhat self-conscious and not a little awed. I may lack the presence of a Paul Carnes, the administrative skills of a Robert West, and the eloquence of a Dana Greeley—at this moment, how I wish for the eloquence of a Dana Greeley!

"What I do bring to the presidency, however, is the conviction that, though we face a crisis, we are not lost. What I do bring is a willingness to experiment, to try new forms and structures, a capacity to encourage each of us to lend our hearts to our precious movement, and a commitment to see that no one is excluded and that individual differences are respected. Indeed in our diversity lie the seeds of our strength. This is some of what I bring, and, in addition, I know how to change the water cooler on 25 Beacon Street's fourth floor!"

This opening statement was vintage Pickett, for while he was willing to reveal his shortcomings through comparisons with UUA presidents of yesteryear, he was also decisive in affirming what he could and would do. The General Assembly gathering knew unmistakably that in Gene Pickett was a president who would be a faithful water-cooler changer day in and day out! That image parallels De Pree's "cadre of water carriers"—leaders willing to do whatever it takes to make their institutions flourish. In his book *Leadership Jazz*, De Pree states it persuasively: "When I think of water carriers, I think of qualities like compassion, humor, a sense of history, the ability to teach and an unshakable commitment to the tribe." Such held true of Gene Pickett as UUA President.

In Pickett's Berry Street Essay, he focused on the central UUA crisis: "In the first year of my presidency, we were faced with an additional crisis. Over the previous ten years our adult membership had declined by 35,000, and our religious education enrollment was down by 65,000. To turn our membership decline around became a top priority. There were, of course, many reasons for the decline. Some of the difficulties had been due to upheavals in the larger society. This was during the turbulent seventies. Most mainline denominations were also declining—even more than we. And we had been fractured by many conflicting interests and causes. We had not dealt very constructively with some of the elements of our diversity. All of this led, I think, to a malaise of the spirit. We were not feeling very good about ourselves as a movement.

"When we first seriously began to raise the issue of growth, we invariably got into the argument about quality versus quantity. Even among the staff this became an issue. Some felt that getting involved in the 'numbers game' would mean neglecting the quality of our faith. I had learned from my experience in Atlanta that this need *not* be an either/or situation. During the time of most rapid growth in Atlanta, the congregation had experienced an excitement and vitality it had never known. The quality and richness of our worship and programming were greatly enhanced. Growth gave us increased resources to draw on and work with. Since this was true for our congregation, I felt it would be true for the

Association. We needed both quantity *and* quality.

"It was also argued that if we had a 'quality faith,' and if we could articulate our message clearly, then the numbers concern would take care of itself. But it was my contention that even if we expressed our message compellingly, and even if we proclaimed the best news around, we would just end up talking to ourselves unless we had a sense of mission. By mission I did not mean a message or mission statement, but rather a compelling concern for propagating our faith (which is the definition of 'mission'), a desire to share, to let other people know why our UU faith is important in our own lives and what it has to offer to others."

In his first "state of the union" talk, committed to putting an end to the decline, Pickett offered this cautious but hopeful watchword: "5,000 more by '84." Numbers weren't his only concern; the Unitarian Universalist movement according to Pickett had lost its religious moorings.

"The deeper malaise lies in our confusion as to what word we have to spread. The old watchwords of liberalism—freedom, reason, and tolerance—worthy though they may be, are simply not catching the imagination of the contemporary world. They describe a process for approaching the religious depths but they testify to no intimate acquaintance with the depths themselves. If we are ever to speak to a new age, we must supplement our seeking with some profound religious finds."

In this first General Assembly address, Pickett also broached one of the hallmark features of his presidency, unflinching commitment to theological pluralism: "Let us provide an atmosphere in which those among us of all theological persuasions—the Christians, the humanists, the existentialists—may fully explore and boldly express their worldviews without defensiveness, belligerence, or dogmatism. For too long, pluralism as a value has received our lip service. Now let pluralism become at last a real source of vitality and strength. Ours will never be one word, but many. Let them be spoken with confidence and vigor. By rights, ours ought to be the richest theological milieu of any denomination in modern experience."

This high-sounding sentiment was validated in Pickett's own spiritual quest. Although he considered himself a religious humanist, he was grounded in existentialism, respected the wisdom of the Jewish and Christian heritages, and remained open to the stirrings of transcendent revelation. He embodied theological pluralism himself, so he could authentically entertain all the wide-ranging viewpoints alive in our diverse denomination.

Rarely did a sermon or talk delivered by Pickett during his presidential years not allude to the centrality and power of facing our human mortality. His 1979 discourse was no exception. He declared: "Afraid that we would find our doctrines wanting, we have fled from the face of death. And any faith which cannot step boldly, trembling, up to death will be a shrinking faith. And yet it need not be so. It hasn't always been so. One of the most moving experiences of my early ministry in Richmond, Virginia, was a visit to an elderly Universalist, ill but alert, in a nursing home. Eager as this young pastor was to provide some comfort, I was startled when, in reply to my question as to whether there was anything I could do for her, she said, 'Nothing for me, Gene,

I'm fine, not scared, all ready. But there is something I want you to do for the other people in this home. Go to every one of them and tell them that there is no hell and reassure them that it will be all right.' And you know I did that and many of the people thanked me, though I suspect the other ministers in the place weren't quite so thankful."

Gene grew up next door to his uncle's funeral parlor, had served as a medical corpsman in the Navy, and remained deeply sensitive to and present with people during their closing hours on earth. He was a pastor at heart, and in sharing this story of our faith's unrepentant hopefulness, he was letting Unitarian Universalists everywhere know that he would aspire to be a caring, personal leader who would remain present for our movement through fair and foul weather.

He also let the Association know that he would talk about money in his administration and "do so straightforwardly and without shame." Fiscal responsibility would be a major theme in Pickett's presidency. He inherited a movement declining in numbers and short of dollars, and he was determined, even if somewhat scared, to improve its adverse condition. He initiated the Friends of the UUA program and the Visions for Growth fund drive, and developed beneficial ties with the Veatch Program of the North Shore Unitarian Universalist Society (NSUUS) in Plandome, New York. Pickett reported that NSUUS had generously established a $20 million endowment fund for the Association, a gift that gave the movement a degree of financial stability it had never known. The Friends of the UUA campaign was unprecedented because it asked individuals for $25 contributions. The UUA had previously solicited financial support only from congregations and from "big givers," never directly from the rank-and-file members. Gene had never been comfortable seeking salary increases for himself during his parish career. Pursuing money on behalf of the larger denomination seemed a nobler, less self-serving task:

"The president must be involved first-hand with fundraising. He must be unafraid to ask and proud to receive. He must go in person, where need be, to preach our cause and reassure our congregants that the organization to which they are being asked to give is vital, prospering, worthy and witnessing in the world. Within six years we can expect to see our Association financially sound. Let this be our common dream."

In 1979, as the result of an unusual and complicated bequest, the UUA began to receive substantial funds from what was known as the Holdeen India Fund. Some of the funds could be used by special Association programs, but the largest proportion was designated for charitable use in India.

The quest for racial justice had been central to Pickett's ministry in the South, and his presidency would be marked by both ringing exhortation and ceaseless labor on behalf of interracial harmony. Every one of his seven presidential addresses emphasized Unitarian Universalism's allegiance to greater racial equity in the world and within its own religious communities. In 1979 he phrased his summons as follows: "We need not remain as lily-white a denomination as we now are. Whether through an affirmative action program for the recruitment of black leadership (which we have already begun) or through a new commission on racial justice with real power to guide our hands and rivet our wandering eyes, or through some other means, we need to call upon the wisdom of our black constituency and call upon the will of all of us, black and white, to make those ancient promises a new reality."

This statement echoed his powerful entreaty at the Unitarian Universalist observance of the twenty-fifth anniversary of *Brown* v. *Board of Education, Topeka, Kansas*, the United States Supreme Court decision that desegregated public schools. On that occasion Pickett remarked: "Twenty-five years later, one thing we do know: that if we expect more black Unitarian Universalists, we must try to demonstrate that we really want them. Passivity, color blindness, or brave proclamations are not enough. We must be held accountable for our acts. We must never let it be said that we didn't even try . . . to broaden our sympathies; speak for the oppressed; invite a heterogeneous confession; and repair our moted eye."

There was no ethical cause for which Pickett labored more vehemently throughout his career than combating racism. As he put it: "If we abandon the struggle for racial justice simply because it no longer is chic; if we give up the quest to attract more people of color to this denomination simply because that road is a hard one; if we give up these goals, we give up our souls."

Pickett in his first year of presidency represented a conciliatory force, too. He pledged to bring our theological schools to a common table, showed interest in developing an alliance of Unitarian Universalist scholars, and openly welcomed the assistance of all former presidents and vice presidents.

He concluded his 1979 General Assembly address with the story of Helen's harrowing accident and how that tragedy had bonded them together as a married couple and reinforced his conviction "that out of darkness life can call forth new blessings. Nothing is ever entirely lost, not at least until the very end and perhaps not even then. I have seen it in my own life and I see it now in ours" as a denomination.

He closed with these words: "So, my friends, these are our tasks and dreams, as I see them. They are both enormous and very simple. And whether or not we meet them all, whether or not we refurbish our finances and find the 5,000, there is one thing I can promise: that we will play it out, if need be to the end, that I will do my best, and one more thing, that 25 Beacon Street's fourth floor will never want for water!"

1980—Albuquerque

At the 1980 General Assembly in Albuquerque, New Mexico, Pickett started the review of his first year in office with the central enigma of his life and presidency—being a cautiously happy person. He said: "One year ago I stood before you not a little anxious. Deep inside, where night thoughts haunt sleep, I had ambivalent feelings about being president. I was not certain that I would even *like* the job. Some of you know that I possess a constitutional aversion to admitting that I am happy. To admit to happiness is dangerous and invites hope to be dashed. Better to remain just a bit dissatisfied and thereby stave off disappointment. Well, I've been fighting it for months, doing my best to keep it at mind's length, but finally I have arrived at the conclusion: I like being president of the UUA and, what's more, I think it's going very well.

"Let me tell you why I like it: in how many jobs could one travel 70,000 miles, appear in sixty-four different towns and deliver 157 speeches, all in twelve months? I ask you: in how many other jobs could one sleep in seventy-six different guest rooms and eat forty-one banquet meals? I ask you: in how many other jobs could one host an average of 1.8 cocktail parties every week one is at home in Boston? I ask you: in how many other jobs could one twice have the experience of being the guest of honor at a reception yet not be introduced?

"For all of you who yearn to be president in future years, I would urge, for your own well being, that you enter a retreat house for a fortnight, taking these statistics as your mantra. Remember: I *like* being president. I just have trouble owning up to happiness!"

Gene then acknowledged the indispensability of Helen as his partner in the presidency: "a person devoted in her own right to the future of our cause, a steady confidante, loving critic, and ever-present companion to whom our movement owes more than it will ever know." With natural devotion Gene would unwaveringly mention, at the start of every General Assembly address, his abiding gratitude for Helen's companionship.

The second person whom he unfailingly lauded was the executive vice president, Bill Schulz: "When I became president, I wanted a full partner in policy-making, a trusted advisor. . . . It has been one of my great joys to find in Bill Schulz a keen imagination, sensitive ear, a close personal friend, a gifted speaker, and one who quickly earned the respect of those who work with him. And, the headquarters is always in one piece when I return from my travels."

Gene reported that "the UUA is approaching a degree of financial stability for the first time in many, many years . . . with the Friends of the UUA campaign succeeding beyond our fondest hopes, having raised over $150,000 and the Annual Program Fund reaching the goal, which is an unprecedented twelve percent higher than the previous year." Other new programs of note that year included the Extension Training Program, the Urban Church Coalition, the UUA Media Feasibility Committee, the Religious Education Futures Committee, and the reconstituting of the entire continental youth organization. He also mentioned the heartening resurgence of Beacon Press, new liturgical materials produced by the Commission on Common Worship, an internal institutional racism audit of the UUA, the start of a revamped General Resolutions process, and creative initiatives proposed by the Women and Religion Committee.

During the year Pickett had addressed the Women and Religion Convocation in East Lansing, Michigan, with forceful conviction: "You are changing the situation of women within our denomination and, in so doing, you are opening up for all of us new ways of understanding and perceiving women and, we hope, men as well. And furthermore, this change is something the church, as an institution, could not do for itself. We might say it is pre-institutional. By changing women's situation within the institution, your impact can be enormous in affecting sexist attitudes, assumptions, and behavior. Let us all resolve to make it so."

In this speech Pickett also shared a family experience that demonstrated how difficult, complex, and often personal it is to put aside traditional assumptions and language: "A year or so ago, my daughter Martha told me she was seriously considering going into the Unitarian Universalist ministry. I was taken by surprise, but after collecting my thoughts I told her I was greatly flattered she was interested in entering this profession which means so much to me. After some further hesitation I admitted that, if I had had a son, the idea of his following in my footsteps would have crossed my mind, but it had never occurred to me that one of my daughters would be interested in being a minister. I tell you this story to demonstrate how very difficult it is for all of us, even the best intentioned, to put aside traditional assumptions about the female role."

Pickett's prophetic emphasis in this 1980 talk focused both on creating a world without war and "rebuffing the emergent new right in its vengeful desire to smother the rights of women, gay people, minorities, and others who struggle for justice." He referred to a statement that he had made recently in Anchorage, Alaska, where he spoke on television in opposition to the Moral Majority that had targeted the local Unitarian Universalists for special censure. Pickett exclaimed: "Freedom is no longer exclusive in our society; it is becoming more and more inclusive: Black rights, Chicano rights, and Indian rights; women's rights and gay rights; workers' rights and veterans' rights; children's rights and students' rights; welfare rights and tenants' rights; the rights of the elderly and the rights of the handicapped. We are at a turning point: from old forms and institutions to new forms and institutions. This makes many people uneasy, fearful. They take refuge in old sanctities, afraid to face a new day. But we must not allow these timid, frightened voices to rule the future. Channing said it many generations ago: 'No firm tread but by going on!'"

Pickett closed his report with a confession: "While I do not consider myself to be a professional theologian, I do believe there is no more important task before us than to take theology seriously once again. Therefore, as one step toward that goal, I plan to institute a President's Symposium on Theological Options at the next General Assembly."

He went on to describe the balanced faith he felt essential for the new generation: "Something on this order—a faith for both the mind *and* the spirit, made out of experience and tradition, heart and soul, not separate but integrated, alive and mutually reinforcing. . . . Authoritarianism in religion is spreading from Iran to Alaska. Unitarian Universalism must offer a viable alternative to authoritarianism—not rationalism alone, for that would be sterile, and not mysticism alone, for that would be mindless—but a powerful combination of the two which asserts that we are less than immortal but more than matter and capable of the most awesome affirmation."

1981—Philadelphia

Pickett commenced his 1981 "state of the union" address in Philadelphia, Pennsylvania, with this reflection: "To have been unchallenged in this election year as I sought a full term as president has been both a humbling and a confirming experience. Saki once observed that 'the young have aspirations which never come to pass; the old have reminiscences of what never happened; only the middle-aged are really conscious of their limitations.'

"Clearly, I am middle-aged, and I am clearly aware of my limitations. But I am also extremely proud of what in two years we have accomplished. And I am also greatly honored that you have enabled me to stand for election for four more years. But greater than the honor to me is the unity which I hope this election will bring to our movement. And believe me, if ever the children of light required unity, it is today. We face challenges, both institutional and public, rare in our history, and it is those to which I want to speak this morning as we begin our twentieth year as a merged Association."

Pickett, as usual, pinpointed highlights of the concluded year. For twelve years the Association had been averaging losses of more than ten societies per year. In 1981 there was a net gain of one—the tide was being reversed, although loss of members had not been stemmed. Furthermore, he was proud yet cautious to announce that thirty-six percent of the professional staff at the UUA were women, and that there was unqualified commitment to gender equity starting at 25 Beacon Street.

During this address Pickett railed again in opposition to the militant threat of the Moral Majority that wanted to impose by legal fiat the name Christian on Unitarian Universalism's diverse society. He was particularly riveting in his admonition: "Well, what does such fear command of Unitarian Universalists? I want to remind us that what is most worthy and most admirable in the long story of humankind has been wrought not by moral majorities but by prophetic minorities; not by the smug and the raucous but by the thoughtful and the faithful . . . bemoan though we do the coming of the new religious right, let us remember that our special job as Unitarian Universalists is now what it has always been—to serve as that ethical and prophetic remnant, itself often the target of derision; that 'moral minority' which takes as its obligation the preservation of memory and the pronouncement of justice."

He continued with palpable passion: "A moral minority which models the way of conviction without arrogance, insight without coercion, and democracy without demagoguery. Amos, Jeremiah, Ezekiel, Elizabeth Cady Stanton, Lucretia Mott, Dorothea Dix, none of these could claim affiliation with moral majorities. They were agents of that truth which transcends numbers. . . . The role of a remnant is to remain faithful to a vision of whole cloth even when the budget for cloth has been slashed to a pittance." It was a galvanizing call for Unitarian Universalists to reclaim the power of their vision and to support it unequivocally with their resources.

At the close of this General Assembly, Pickett was installed as UUA president for a second term. Here were his brief yet discerning remarks: "A little more than two years ago, I was chosen president of our Association. By this time during GA week, that seems like ten years ago, at other times it feels like yesterday. But no matter how long it feels, my selection as president *always feels* like an honor—the greatest public honor I have ever known. The office of president carries with it not only the responsibilities of the moment but, in addition, the mantle of history. It is in some sense an embodiment of our Association's highest aspirations.

"My pledge to you is that for these four coming years I take as my personal watchword this ancient declaration: 'Justice, I call to thee. Courage, I nourish thee. Love, I cherish thee.' Let me not fail you, but, even more, let me not fail these!"

1982—Brunswick

It is not surprising that the paramount theme of Pickett's annual address in Brunswick, Maine, was what he called the "Theology of Reversal," for it was central to Gene's philosophy of existence that "an institution can reverse decline, an individual can surmount despair, and the world can overcome evil with righteousness." Never was his theology made so luminous and compelling as during this memorable address.

The longer Pickett stood in the presidency, the more comfortable he became both with his leadership position and in revealing portions of his personal odyssey. Thus, he started his 1982 GA review with a story: "I became a minister thirty years ago for many reasons, but one of them was that I simply could not carry a tune. This inadequacy was impressed upon me early in life when, in the sixth grade, I was denied a place in the class chorus. Can you imagine how painful and humiliating it was in the sixth grade not even to be able to sing 'Sailing, sailing, over the bounding main'?

"This inadequacy resurfaced in theological school, where I was actually required to take voice lessons in order that my 'singing' not throw my congregation off key when I led them in hymns. (I will refrain from providing you the opportunity to judge whether the lessons took or not!) This musical ineptitude has plagued me through the years, and even today I am self-conscious in group singing and will sometimes only mouth the words if I think someone is listening.

"And yet, though I never could carry a tune, on those few occasions when I did appear as a child in a musical program, the adults always congratulated me on my diction. 'He murders the melody,' I imagine they would say to my mother, 'but at least we can understand the words.' Obviously, they were searching for the gold beneath the dross. And you know, it worked! For out of my embarrassment at a tin ear arose the conviction that I might possess, if not a silver tongue, then at least a serviceable one. And so I joined debating societies instead of choruses. I sought parts in class plays rather than in operettas. And though I would never become a choir director, I might become a minister. Out of my childhood pain emerged an adult desire. What had been a failure was turned around, transformed, reversed."

The year before, Pickett was able to announce minimal growth (by one) in UU congregations. In 1982, for the first time in over a decade, there was a net increase in the number of adult Unitarian Universalists. Extension work was bearing some fruit. There was also progress in response to the racism audit reflected in an affirmative action program for hiring people of color, with at least one person of color (and in several cases more than one) sitting on virtually every major UUA committee. Additionally, at fourteen percent, the Unitarian Universalist ministry registered the largest percentage of settled women ministers of all mainline denominations. Gender and racial justice continued to be prophetic imperatives throughout the Pickett presidency. He exhorted people to remember that "justice rolls down like a mighty water, and though such water be temporarily blocked, it can *never* be halted."

For several years the administration had made an intensive effort to strengthen ecumenical relationships, collaborating with a number of religious coalitions working in the areas of economic justice, disarmament, and peace. Reversal was also at work in the deepening of international contacts, particularly in India where the International Association for Religious Freedom (IARF) and the Unitarian Universalist Service Committee (UUSC) labored cooperatively in programs of self-empowerment. A major effort was also undertaken to increase the visibility of Unitarian Universalism through a reorganization of communications and public relations efforts. The latter turned out to be one of the least successful areas during the Pickett years.

Pickett continued to address the threat of nuclear war with robust language drawn from the Universalist heritage: "How appropriate it would be for us Unitarian Universalists on our own twenty-first birthday to reenter the theological fray, to remember in particular our Universalist heritage and to proclaim that, just as a benevolent God could never sanction hell after death, so such a God could never sanction hell on earth and that those who flirt with nuclear war in the name of God flirt thereby with blasphemy!"

1983—Vancouver

Every one of Pickett's presidential addresses echoed his wintry spirituality and emphasized the theme of hope through arduous struggle. The 1983 General Assembly in Vancouver, British Columbia, was no exception. As usual he began with an anecdote of humorous self-disclosure.

"There are advantages to seeing with only one eye. As most of you are aware, I underwent surgery six weeks ago to repair a partially detached retina. The surgery was successful, but for another few weeks I will continue without the use of my right eye. That explains the black patch which I am wearing. But, as I have said, there are advantages to all this. For one, though I have never thought of myself as possessing machismo, for example, it has been rather exhilarating to be constantly compared to Moshe Dayan and the Hathaway shirt-man.

"For another, my visual handicap provides a perfect excuse if I should stumble in the delivery of my speech this morning, which would be unfortunate for you, for my report is rather long. Then, too, it is comforting to know that, though I am seeing only the half of you who are sitting to the left of my nose, I can safely take it on faith that there are actually twice as many Unitarian Universalists here as it appears. If only we could feel such assurance about our membership statistics! I do want you to know, however, that my eye problem, was in no way a function of stress or overwork. It is a not uncommon sequel to cataract surgery, which I had five years ago. Indeed, I thrive on my job."

The greatest achievement during the 1982 to 1983 year was the announcement by the North Shore Unitarian Universalist Society of Plandome, New York, of an $11 million fund for theological education and a $2 million grant to supplement the pension incomes of retired ministers and their spouses. The generosity of the Plandome congregation, thanks to rigorous cultivation by Pickett, continued unabated.

The UUA's growth picture see-sawed: there was a net gain of congregations and a net loss of members in that year. However, there were some "promising hard facts": congregations were doing more building and renovating of their facilities than ever before; parishes in the extension ministry program were growing by over eleven percent each year; urban churches were growing stronger; and, for the first time in fifteen years a consultant was hired to start new UU societies across the continent.

The growth of Unitarian Universalism, according to Pickett, was still "severely hampered by limited resources." In response to this need, he had been planning for several years a capital funds program called Visions for Growth. The goal was $4 to 5 million, and the campaign continued for the remainder of Pickett's presidency. The appeal targeted approximately 500 individuals within the movement.

One of the most important appointments of 1983 proved to be the new director of Beacon Press, Wendy Strothman, who succeeded in making it the most outstanding small publisher of liberal religious studies in North America. Beacon Press was already the leading publisher of feminist theology.

The highly significant Principles and Purposes project, urged by Women and Religion advocates, appeared before the plenary body of the 1983 General Assembly; twenty of the thirty-two recommendations of the UUA's institutional racism audit had been implemented. It was also at this time that Pickett said, "it is my goal, before my term as president ends in 1985, that a task force to draft a new Unitarian Universalist hymnal will have been appointed and begun its work." Additionally, Pickett exhorted congregations over the coming year to "undertake study groups to formulate a liberal religious theology of peacemaking."

He then proceeded to announce the creation of the Unitarian Universalist Peace Network to focus associational efforts in this area. "Ideally, our work for peace will grow out of our religious principles and resonate with the witness of our nonviolent forebears: the Polish Socinians, some of whom refused to bear arms; the Universalist Adin Ballou whose utopian community in Hopedale, Massachusetts, inspired generations of peacemakers; and the Unitarian John Haynes Holmes who challenged another Unitarian, former President William Howard Taft, on the appropriateness of the United States' entry into the First World War. Our heritage commands us to respond to the rule of death, which alike in national and international decisions, plagues our planet."

As was Pickett's custom, he closed his summary of yearly accomplishments and challenges with a personal religious statement. This year it was his magnificent "wintry spirituality" piece, which conveyed the governing theology of his life and work. For those General Assembly listeners who were wintry types it struck a responsive chord; for the summery ones, it drove many to wondering whether Gene had slipped into another depression.

He explained that there were three primary wellsprings of his own ministry: "Helen, whose love and support have remained constant despite the ups and downs of family life and career; second, several psychiatrists whose insights and presence helped keep me centered in both good and difficult times; and a number of caring and worshiping UU communities that both supported and challenged me in my religious pilgrimage."

He elucidated his spiritual journey in these terms: "My search for spiritual nurture has taken me in many directions. Indeed, the longing for such nurture has most frequently been unrequited. I have experienced the absence of God more than the presence of God. But the searching has never ceased. I have tried Zen and Transcendental Meditation, encounter groups and T-groups. But still, there remains an unfulfilled longing.

"And yet I know, I feel, within the very depths of my being that there is a fountainhead, an animating source, a wellspring that nurtures and renews, reveals and affirms. I have pondered that such experiences are most intense at times of loneliness, rejection, pain and uncertainty—at times when bleakness grips my soul."

So for the first time publicly, Pickett was unmistakable in acknowledging his wintry spirituality. He had written frequently on loneliness and death in "Pickett Lines," and his previous General Assembly addresses often accented the theme of comeback, but this was his first self-conscious, extended description of his religious foundations. He had arrived at this defining insight through a passage by the German theologian Karl Rahner, who was quoted in Martin

Marty's book, *The Cry of Absence*. Rahner refers to wintry spirituality as a faith posture that grapples boldly with uncertainty and ambiguity, with pain and loneliness, and with the mystery of death in order to discover meaning and hope. Needless to say, affirmation and assurance are hard-won gifts for the wintry type.

The counterpart is a summery spirituality characterized by assurance and joy, exuberance and warmth. It is more emotional and charismatic and encompasses the dominant form of spirituality. Nevertheless, Pickett noted that the two types do not exclude each other, both are valid, and he advocated recognition of the wintry sort because it is devalued in our American culture.

Rahner's fruitful distinction is reminiscent of philosopher William James's classic division between "once-born" and "twice-born" souls. The former are persons who sail through life rarely experiencing anything that devastates, even complicates, their beliefs and the latter are persons who see the universe as filled, not with sunshine, but shadows, and are burdened with a less than cheerful or confident perspective.

Pickett used these words: "My reason for sharing this with you is to suggest that the wintry sort of spirituality is descriptive of many Unitarian Universalists. There are many of us who may be spiritual without knowing it."

He appropriately concluded with a quote from one of his wintry spirituality cohorts, W. H. Auden: "In the desert of the heart, let the healing fountains start. In the prison of our days, teach us freely how to praise!"

1984—Columbus

Given his temperament, it is no surprise that Maine humor was appealing to Pickett ever since his arrival in New England in 1974. He began his 1984 address in Columbus, Ohio, with a typical Mainiac story: "During the first months of my presidency I began many of my speeches with a story from the state of Maine. Maine humor is rather specialized, and many people do not appreciate or even understand it. Some people will laugh at a well-done Maine accent even if they don't grasp the point of the story. But a Maine story without a Maine accent is especially risky as an opening gambit. But I persisted even though audiences did not respond well. After a year or so I gave it up, but this morning I have decided to try it one more time.

"The story has to do with a Maine couple who, after a restful night's sleep, rose early to prepare for a new day. The wife proceeded to the kitchen to make breakfast, and the husband went outdoors to savor the beautiful morning. The sky was clear and blue, and the sun shone brightly. It was Maine weather at its best. Shortly, the husband returned to the kitchen and said to his wife, 'Well, Mary, we are really going to have to pay for this.'

"Just as I feared, still few laughs. I'm sorry, because it's not only a good Maine story but it also has a good Puritan moral, and this is that for anything good or pleasurable we experience we have to pay an unpleasant penalty in return. It was this attitude which colored my feelings about the Association during my first years as president. Everything was going so well that something untoward was bound to happen. It was like waiting for the other shoe to fall. And here it is five years later; my term as president is almost over, and the Association is still doing very well. The shoe has not fallen."

After acknowledging former UUA President Dana McLean Greeley, who was attending his fifty-ninth consecutive General Assembly and who began attending the very year Gene was conceived, Pickett proceeded to summarize briefly all that had been accomplished during the past five years, "not because I personally take credit for it all, but because I think it is a story that should make every one of us feel proud."

He recounted the growth in adult members and reported a six percent increase in the number of children enrolled in religious education programs. He announced the charting of a new direction in religious education curriculum development; a $9 million endowment fund for theological education; expanded field services and increased training opportunities for lay leaders; the transformative impact of the Women and Religion movement; the new statement of Purposes and Principles to be adopted at the 1985 General Assembly; a revision of the resolutions process to be in place for the 1986 General Assembly; a "social action program which has remained high on our denominational agenda during my presidency, sometimes to the dismay of some"; the emergence of IARF as an important forum for dialogue among major religions of the world; and the fact that "the Association is stronger financially than it has ever been in our history."

At the 1984 General Assembly, Pickett spoke less of secular social challenges and more of the changes that would make Unitarian Universalism a more effective liberal religious movement. He said: "We must break out of the petty parochialisms that sap our energies and distort our vision. Not many years have passed since one could sense a malaise in our movement that was characterized by distrust, pessimism, and cynicism. We had lost our sense of optimism and hope, our sense of being part of something significant and exciting, something greater than our own personal concerns or our own local societies. Yet parochialism is still strong within our movement. But I feel this is changing, too.

"If we are to save this planet from destruction, more and more of us are going to have to sense 'we're all in it together.' If we are to revitalize a sense of liberal religious community, more and more of us are going to have to sense 'we're all in it together.' The future of Unitarian Universalism as a movement has always been more precious to me than my own personal career or local church. And from the very beginning of my presidency, I have been convinced that only in partnership can we build a strong and vital religious movement. Only if we are all in it together can we build our version of the promised land here. And this is what partnership is built upon: honest discussion, respectful disagreement, sometimes painful compromise, and some times joyous reconciliation."

Pickett gently rebuked the assembly for sometimes nullifying their own power by pushing from opposite sides of the same heavy load: "Power lies in balancing our varying needs, in honoring our diverse feelings, and in reconciling our differences so that we may move forward together." He was targeting the fact that rugged individualism must give way to manifestations of the "interdependent web" in both the fundamental philosophy and pragmatic functioning of the Unitarian Universalist Association.

This same theme was eloquently reinforced in a sermon he delivered later that year at the Second Church in Chicago: "Because we are individualists, we tend to distrust our institutions. Because we are congregationalists, we tend to support associative action reluctantly. Because we are nonconformists, we tend to resist the lessons of the past, many of which warn us of mistaking rhetoric for substance and embracing an arrogant, if not excessive, individualism which can be destructive of the common good.

"Unitarian Universalism is an idea, a faith, an international movement, an historical institution whose expression is more than congregational, but other than hierarchical. The key word is *associative*. We work and worship in association with one another, which is to say, in partnership with one another. The Association represents our best effort to walk together in trust and respect with all who value a free but organized religion."

Pickett closed his presentation with an affecting illustration from his own religious development: "During my growing-up years in a small village in Maryland, the local Methodist church was central in my life. But in my high school years, questions and doubts about my religious beliefs began to surface. Feelings of isolation began to grow, for there was no one with whom I could discuss my changing beliefs and experiences, no one to share my yearning and searching. My high school and early college days and my time in the Navy were deeply lonely times. I still recall with painful intensity those early months in the Navy when I was eighteen, frightened, and alone.

"At the end of the day, I would crawl into my bunk, pull the blankets over my head, and pray that God or someone would help me in my loneliness, and then I would cry myself to sleep, fearful that someone in a nearby bunk would hear me. Praying didn't seem to help, but I think the crying did. How much I wanted someone to share my religious search. How great was my need for someone to care.

"The need for a supportive and searching religious community has never left me. That, in part, is why I became a minister. That, in part, is why I am committed to building a strong Unitarian Universalist movement. And more important than the bylaws, stronger than the structure, deeper, much deeper than the politics, is the feeling that 'we're all in it together,' and that our loving confrontation and our honest caring can only make us stronger. In the words of James Baldwin, 'the moment we cease to hold each other, the moment we break faith with one another, the sea engulfs us and the light goes out.' It is my fervent prayer that the light shall shine forever."

1985—Atlanta

It was a sentimental coincidence that the 1985 General Assembly was held in Atlanta, Georgia. That is where Pickett concluded his parish ministry in 1974, and now he was completing his tour of duty as UUA president in the same city.

In a worship service at the Atlanta congregation on the

Sunday preceding Gene's last General Assembly, he divulged these sentiments: "I loved this space, this congregation, this building. Atlanta is where I knew my greatest satisfaction as a minister and where I experienced my deepest despair as a person. Atlanta is where I learned ministry is a mutual relationship—I learned as much from you as you ever learned from me. Atlanta is where Helen and I made some of our closest friendships."

During his "state of the union," Gene once more summarized the major hallmarks of his term in office and closed by saying that he would "like most to be remembered for my part in inspiring growth and the renewal of spirit in our movement." In truth, during the Pickett years the Association's shrinking membership had reversed itself. The number of new congregations had grown by seventy-three, and the number of children attending religious education classes had increased as well. There was also a major strengthening of the UUA's finances through a greatly augmented endowment (from $9 million to over $40 million), expanded giving to the Annual Program Fund, and a dramatic increase in individual generosity since the establishment of the Friends of the UUA and the Visions for Growth programs.

"Gene did not start all these things," ventured one UUA official, "but his quiet diplomacy, his perseverance, and his faith in the potential for growth of our denomination have caused significant advances in these areas." Gene, playing down his own talent with a gentle laugh, gave some credit to Protestant fundamentalism for its role in Unitarian Universalism's growth.

Despite Pickett's personal shyness and protestations, on

May 31, 1985, Bill Holway, the UUA Director of Extension, presented Gene with a grand honor with respect to his unbending commitment to the expansion of the Unitarian Universalist gospel. Holway remarked in part: "You have been the source of inspiration and encouragement which has turned around our decline and renewed our growth, individually and institutionally. You offered us both a vision and a challenge, saying, 'Won't you join me, come along!'

"So, while in person, as president, you will not be leading us, we've decided to 'institutionalize' your spirit, that you may continue to lead us, challenge us, empower us to spread the good word of Unitarian Universalism on into the future.

"In order to do this, the Extension Section is establishing an award in your honor. Tonight we are proud to announce the creation of the O. Eugene Pickett Award, which will be presented annually to a congregation that has made an outstanding contribution to the growth of Unitarian Universalism. Nominations will be made by districts, with the nominee of each district recognized, and the continental winner presented an award at General Assembly. . . . Through this award, may you continue to call us forward to the best that we might be."

In a letter of tribute at the close of Pickett's tenure, ministerial colleague Peter Raible offered his perspective: "You came to office under difficult circumstances: Paul's death and a narrow board vote. The fact that from the very beginning you have moved so forcefully and with such wide approval indicates your talents. You leave a much beloved president.

"Yet, far more important, you have carried the weight of

office ever in a human manner. Often bone-weary, sometimes discouraged, occasionally defeated, you have never lost your humane qualities. In short, you have never been captured by the office. I can think of no higher testament to the person you are. 'Well done thou good and faithful servant.'"

One of the recurrent social responsibility themes of Pickett's presidency was racial justice. He revisited this theme in his "state of the union" speech: "convinced that the Unitarian message of reason and the free mind combined with the Universalist message of love and hope can have compelling appeal for thousands who are not white, middle class, and college educated. While we have succeeded in reaching people of diverse beliefs, we have failed to connect with women and men of diverse color and backgrounds." That, for Pickett, remained a preeminent challenge for the coming administration.

Another pressing mandate for the next president would be to serve as a compelling public spokesperson for Unitarian Universalism. "My successor must use every vehicle at his or her command to bring our liberal religious message to the attention of the world." A final concern, contended Pickett, was for people to "reconstitute a Unitarian Universalism of substance and inspiration. There is a great yearning for a serious probing of the depth dimension of our faith. We must speak to the quality of our religious experience, the meaning of existence."

Considering his presidency as a form of ministry, Pickett thanked the manifold people who had collaborated with him during his term: "As the late Casey Stengel said after the New York Yankees had won still another baseball championship:

'I could hardly have done it without the players.' These years as president have made me deeply aware of how much we need one another. Two essential elements of my style of leadership have been a keen sense of mutual need and caring and a shared sense of responsibility. I have been very much aware of how dependent I am on others, on many of you, for cooperation and counsel, for support and encouragement in times of both failure and success."

He went on to amplify his philosophy of creative dependence: "If dependence is the only binding aspect of a relationship, it can result in weakness and even destructiveness. But for the most part the acknowledgment of my dependence has resulted in a greater openness to others, a deeper sense of mutuality and an expanded sense of self that frees me to absorb the energy, the perspectives, and the insights of others."

He closed his final General Assembly address with a story from John Bunyan's *Pilgrim's Progress*, accenting the differences between the two allegorical characters Mr. Valiant-for-Truth, who represents unbridled individualism, and Mr. Ready-to-Halt, who is lame and unable to walk without crutches. Gene clearly identified with Mr. Ready-to-Halt who reaches the river on his journey only with the assistance of others.

Mr. Ready-to-Halt speaks in a quiet yet firm voice: "These crutches I bequeath to the one who shall follow in my steps, with a hundred warm wishes that my successor may prove better than I have done." Gene added his own voice: "And so, like him, I bequeath to you and to my successor my crutches and a hundred warm wishes that the future will be better than anything we have known."

A Larger Ministry

"I would not give a fig for the simplicity this side
of complexity, but I would give my life for the
simplicity on the other side of complexity."

Justice Oliver Wendell Holmes

Church of the Larger Fellowship

After retiring from the UUA presidency, the Picketts decided
that they would each work for five or six more years, and
then retire. For Gene, the choices were to serve as a settled
or interim minister, or to assume leadership of an organization like the Church of the Larger Fellowship (CLF).

Pickett was serving on the CLF board when several board
members asked him if he would be interested in pursuing
this ministry. They were working out a sabbatical plan for
the current minister, George Marshall, who planned to retire upon his return. The timing was awkward for Pickett
who had a year's sabbatical coming after his own term as
president of the UUA. He told CLF board members that he
would be interested if there could be an interim between
Marshall's departure and his own arrival. The politics of the
transition became unpleasant when it appeared to some like

an inside job, and pressure was placed on Pickett to forfeit his sabbatical year, a sacrifice he refused to make. Two of the wisest professional decisions Pickett ever made were to seize his sabbaticals, the first one, near the end of his ministry in Atlanta; the second one, following his tenure as UUA president. He had earned them both.

Helen and Gene talked about traveling around the world, visiting places they had never seen, but quickly realized that they were both bone-weary. They decided to move to Cape Cod, settle in, and see if that location would work as a potential retirement site for them. So they migrated to the Cape, and apart from modest trips, simply unwound for a year.

After the sabbatical Pickett began his ministry at CLF in Boston. The financial condition of the organization was nearly bankrupt, and it owed a large sum of money to the UUA, yet the executive position met several of Gene's primary objectives: to remain in Boston, utilize his administrative and pastoral gifts, have some relief from the pressure of a higher-powered job, and have the opportunity to toil together with Helen, this time with both in paid positions. Serving as the receptionist and as Gene's administrative assistant, Helen proved adept at engaging people on the phone or in person, "a real live information center." The Picketts enjoyed working together and collaborating with a congenial staff.

CLF provided a sufficiently intriguing challenge, and enabled Gene to use his experience and contacts in a way both helpful to CLF and satisfactory to himself. It also allowed the Picketts to live both on Beacon Hill and Cape Cod. Transforming CLF into a viable enterprise was a task that necessitated an organizational and programmatic overhaul. When Gene arrived, CLF was administratively disorganized, housed in basement offices provided by the UUA, $100,000 in debt to the UUA, and operating at a $40,000 deficit every year. In two years, Pickett and his competent staff had inaugurated a well-organized, every-member canvas, installed computers, restructured personnel, reduced the UUA debt substantially, and produced a balanced budget. The format of the newsletter, *Quest*, was altered, and fresh outreach programs were initiated.

Pickett employed his connections throughout the Unitarian Universalist world to garner support and obtain grants to restabilize CLF. Nevertheless, staying in Boston and working so closely with the UUA administration was a mixed blessing. CLF was frequently included in administration staff meetings and social gatherings, and Gene never quite felt comfortable there because of the change in his role in relation to the staff.

The organization functioned so well that Pickett eventually needed an assistant. It was mutual good fortune that the Reverend Scott Alexander was available and well matched with the open position. Alexander brought eagerness and vitality to the team. As Helen put it: "Gene has always attracted high-energy friends" who furnished a counterweight to his quiet enthusiasm. He wasn't jealous of that energy, but welcomed it as a complementary gift.

Gene conceived the mission of CLF as serving two functions: first, to minister to its membership of over 2,000 isolated UU individuals and families and, second, to operate as an extension program for our movement, since many programs were equally adaptable for small society use and enrichment. CLF was successful on both counts. Each year, CLF would place over 500 names on their introductory mailing list, and, of these, twenty-one percent became members. During Gene's tour of duty, the organization averaged about two hundred and fifty new members a year.

International Association for Religious Freedom

During his time as minister of CLF, Gene also served as president of the International Association for Religious Freedom (IARF), an international, interfaith organization founded by the American Unitarian Association one hundred years before. This role became a major responsibility because there was a changing of the guard with the retirement of Diether Gehrmann.

Gehrman had served as general secretary for eighteen years and had led the IARF through a period of creative change and unprecedented growth. He had been responsible for broadening its membership and building a strong and vital organization. The member groups had increased in number from 33 to 56 and represented most of the major faith traditions in the world. Diether had taken a floundering enterprise, centered largely in Europe and North America, with an office no larger than a church closet, and guided, pushed, and pulled it into a healthy, viable, international, interfaith organization. With these accomplishments to Diether's credit, the IARF Council felt that this would be a propitious time for him to retire. Because no provision for retirement had been made, Pickett took the lead in assembling a generous retirement package, funded mainly by the Japanese and the North Americans.

Until Gene became UUA president, he knew little about the international connections of liberal religion, but his worldwide travels profoundly expanded his perspective. He learned that the unfettered, hopeful faith of Unitarian Universalism had appeal beyond upper-middle class whites on the North American continent.

Pickett came to feel that since North American Unitarian Universalists were the strongest and most affluent strand of this worldwide religious movement, they had a responsibility to share with those less favored. Pickett was roundly appreciated for his steadfast support of Unitarian Universalism's often-struggling spiritual kin in other lands. C. Lyngdoh, executive secretary of the Khasi Hills Unitarian churches in India, wrote a note of gratitude to Pickett upon his retirement saying: "As regards your relationship with the Khasi Unitarians and the Indian Unitarians, permit me to say that you are regarded as our Elder Brother, who is always lending a helping hand to those who need your help and support. . . . We offer a prayer for your health and happiness. May God be with you and your wife Helen during the rest of your life."

Pickett was impressed by the inordinate courage displayed in Transylvania where the Unitarians had been persecuted for hundreds of years while still retaining their vital heritage. Although the theology of Unitarians and Universalists in other lands was universally more Christian-oriented than in North America, people shared an abiding commonality with western Unitarian Universalists. They were committed to a generous tolerance, and the concept of one God remained a dynamic, unifying force for these people.

Where Dana Greeley had thrived on ceremonious bonds and royal exchanges, especially with the Japanese in the Rissho Kosei-kai, and with President Niwano, Gene felt awkward and out of place meeting the prime ambassadors of religious and cultural organizations. He more comfortably engaged the second rung of leaders who reached shared decisions out of the limelight.

Pickett considered the IARF to be a unique and important worldwide interfaith organization that furnished a significant bond between East and West. It was Gene's hope that "we will continue to expand our membership so as to include an even broader spectrum of theological and philosophical positions. We need to have stronger representation from Jewish, humanist, Christian, and Moslem traditions. And if we are to be a truly worldwide religious association, we need more representation from Africa and Latin America. Such broadening of our membership would certainly enrich and deepen the religious life of the IARF. It would also bear witness to the world that unity in diversity is possible and that religious difference can be a source of strength rather than a source of conflict."

The Consummate Reward

On June 25, 1989 at the General Assembly in New Haven, Connecticut, Pickett received the highest accolade achievable in Unitarian Universalist ranks: the Award for Distinguished Service to the Cause of Unitarian Universalism. His acceptance speech echoes some of the enduring themes of his relationship with this chosen faith community: "Thank you for this recognition and this very great honor and for the thoughtful and kind words inscribed on this award. As usual, I am convinced that anyone but me would be able to respond with some clever or humorous remark that would lighten the solemnity of this occasion.

"Now, if I were in the position of giving awards, I would give my Most Enduring Influence Award to Unitarian Universalism. For this movement has influenced, enriched, and blessed me in ways far beyond measure. From the time I discovered Unitarianism at the All Souls Unitarian Church in Washington, DC, to the present, it has been this movement and this Association that have given purpose and form to my life and work."

After briefly recounting his religious upbringing and evolution, he extended a familiar yet challenging refrain to the General Assembly: "The longer I am a part of this movement, the more convinced I become that the values and ideals of liberal religion can be effective only if they have a solid institutional base, and that means strong congregations and a strong Association. I know that we as a religious movement have traditionally been suspicious of a strong Association. We have been fearful that strength would mean power, rigidity, and control. But I am convinced that our Association can be both strong and flexible, an institution of which we can be critical while still being committed to it.

"We tend to be a contentious group of people. We are often harder on ourselves than are our fundamentalist critics. It is so easy to be cynical and mistrustful. But the UUA is what binds us together. It is a vehicle of our hope.

"Those years as president made me deeply aware of how

much we need one another. It is only as we recognize our mutuality, honor our diversity, and reconcile our differences with respectful honesty that we can build a strong and vital religious community. Being part of and nurturing such a religious community is what ministry is to me. . . .

"I have found that I need *you* in order to be *me*, that we need *them* in order to be *us*, that only *together* do we have a future. Could we but accept and act on this simple but basic insight, prejudices would be undermined, injustices denounced, and exploitation of nature and people condemned. The world would become *ours* and all women and men *us*.

"This honor has caused me to reflect on my life and ministry. I empathize with the feelings Aldous Huxley expressed when he wrote, 'It's a bit embarrassing to have been concerned with the human problem all one's life and find at the end that one has no more to offer by the way of advice than this: try to be a little kinder.' And so may we be a little kinder. Thank you."

Homestretch

> "Call it grace, call it mystery, call it possibility,
> but all Unitarian Universalist faiths must meet
> the dying light with lips shaping just one word:
> eternal, immutable YES!"
>
> O. Eugene Pickett

Leader Still

When the Picketts finally retired from their joint CLF responsibilities in 1991, Gene assumed that in a relaxed situation he might do some essay writing. Without specific thought of publishing, he simply wanted "to reconstruct my life and career." He bought a number of books about writing, but has not opened them to this day.

Helen, in looking back, attests, "Working on the hymnbook was the most wonderful thing that ever happened to me with the exception of marrying Gene and raising our children." She was a member of the UUA Hymnbook Resources Commission during the five years she worked at CLF. Helen had been involved in church music all her life, had helped organize choirs in all three of their parishes, and knew the denomination well. "I felt prepared and equipped and had a special contribution to make. It was absolutely the right assignment for me, a peak experience," she says. Gene is especially pleased to have his responsive reading entitled "We Give Thanks This Day" nestled in "Helen's hymnbook," because he considers the written word an enduring legacy.

We Give Thanks This Day
For the expanding grandeur of Creation, worlds known and unknown, galaxies beyond galaxies, filling us with awe and challenging our imaginations:

We give thanks this day.

For this fragile planet earth, its times and tides, its sunsets and seasons:

We give thanks this day.

For the joy of human life, its wonders and surprises, its hopes and achievements:

We give thanks this day.

For our human community, our common past and future hope, our oneness transcending all separation, our capacity to work for peace and justice in the midst of hostility and oppression:

We give thanks this day.

For high hopes and noble causes, for faith without fanaticism, for understanding of views not shared:

We give thanks this day.

For all who have labored and suffered for a fairer world, who have lived so that others might live in dignity and freedom:

We give thanks this day.

For human liberty and sacred rites; for opportunities to change and grow, to affirm and choose:

We give thanks this day. We pray that we may live not by our fears but by our hopes, not by our words but by our deeds.

Thus, Gene's words are interwoven in *Singing the Living Tradition* just as Helen's photo was included in Gene's presidential portrait.

Being a superlative, inveterate administrator, Pickett assumed further leadership posts as chair of the Denominational Grants Panel, then chair of the Meadville/Lombard Theological School board, and finally as a co-director of Carolyn Owen-Towle's campaign for the UUA presidency in 1993. Owen-Towle and Gene met while serving together on the board of Meadville/Lombard Theological School. Pickett felt strongly that it was time for a woman to be president of the UUA, and that Owen-Towle, with her denominational credentials as a proven leader, would be the right person. He posed the question to her, and Owen-Towle was unwilling to say "yes" at the time. Months later, however, she called Pickett and said, "I will run, Gene, if you are willing to chair the campaign." He responded rapidly with his own "yes," but felt that there ought to be two campaign directors and suggested Drusilla Cummins, a veteran associational leader and life-long Universalist.

The continental campaign committee grew, with Dr. James Luther Adams and Dr. Gwendolyn Thomas emerging as honorary co-chairs. Carolyn, Gene, and Drusilla soon realized that they needed additional campaign assistance, so the name of Robert Hohler, an established public relations professional was proposed. Hohler had worked on the UUA staff in the past, was an ardent Black Affairs Council supporter during the 1960s, and also served as director of the Layman's League. He even ran for president of the Unitarian Universalist Association at one point, but had dropped out of the denominational picture until he became

Pickett with former board of trustee member Winnie Norman at General Assembly.

reinvolved through work with the Unitarian Universalist Service Committee, and later with William Schulz's presidential campaign.

Gene and Helen were delighted to reenter the denominational fray and were earnestly committed to Carolyn's candidacy. Pickett was acting on his cardinal principles and beliefs in promoting her path of leadership. His campaign advocacy offered excitement and challenge as well as personal satisfaction in reconnecting with ministers and laity with whom he had not conversed in years. It was a vicarious experience for Gene, because he himself would never have felt comfortable campaigning so rigorously, so vulnerably, and so interminably. He felt tremendous empathy for Carolyn, remarking, "A full-fledged, contested election is certainly not something I would have ever put myself through." A few of the old-guard ministers, who felt it was bad form for a former president to demonstrate active support for a candidate, expressed disgruntlement, but the vast majority had no problem with his involvement.

Gene contends that the election was lost at General Assembly, where more people than in previous elections arrived undecided. He assessed that first-time delegates, even though many of them were women, were unwilling to negotiate the radical changes implied in supporting Owen-Towle. Despite Owen-Towle's narrow defeat, Pickett never experienced any personal regret in steering the campaign."

In summing up his feelings after the loss, Gene said, "Helen and I both share in the deep disappointment about the barely missed opportunity for Carolyn Owen-Towle to provide her inclusive style of leadership for our movement—

leadership that I believe would have made a significant difference for us all. I still marvel at the courage Carolyn exhibited in making the run for the presidency. Though she did not win, I am confident that her commendable effort will have a continuing, positive influence on Unitarian Universalism."

On the Cape

The Picketts have maintained a modicum of denominational participation since the 1993 election, Helen serving on the CLF board and Gene on the Ministerial Fellowship Committee. They are also becoming involved in their local UU church in Barnstable, Massachusetts. For Helen, this is the first time she has ever been a member of a church where neither her father nor her husband was the minister.

In their East Sandwich home, Gene thrives on the quiet, bucolic environment. Even background music soon becomes a distraction to his solitude. He is happy in retirement to spend tranquil days alongside Helen, with occasional visits from his adult daughters and their families. Whereas Gene was often miserable as a loner growing up, now he takes sweet refuge in a world relatively free of people, pressure, and tasks. He and Helen have balanced their relationship to appreciate times alone and together. They certainly do not long for the heavy, compulsive stimulation that marked their earlier days. They are good putterers, following their noses, doing this and that, some gardening, bird-watching, reading, traveling, and sauntering—content, never bored.

All who know Gene remark about his dry, subtle sense

of wit. He tells jokes rarely, because he has trouble remembering them. In his sermons he would elicit chuckles most frequently from his mispronunciations and assorted fumbles, and he would willingly join in on the laughter. He still pokes easy fun at himself. And now, in retirement, he sports a knowing, comfortable smile.

The Picketts are simplifying their lives and are content with the measured pace and balance. They are also shedding things and pruning tasks as they contemplate moving to a retirement village. Gene describes this turn in the road as follows: "I have no deep driving desire left. I don't have a sense that there's something I must do before I die. I am quite at ease with what I have said and what I have done. I have been richly rewarded, and feel a sense of accomplishment in realizing so much of my potential that I never imagined I would realize. Our marriage has evolved into a very good, satisfying, deep relationship and, in a real sense, Pickett House will serve as my tombstone up there at 25.

"In the ministry I would sometimes counsel people who had waited too long before determining their future residence. They slowly but surely lost control of their lives, folded up their tent, and died. I want to make my retirement decisions intentionally and not leave matters up to family members or friends. I want us to navigate our moves while we are still in charge of our destinies."

Consequently, the Picketts have explored their options. They want their final residence to be where the geography and weather are pleasant; a vital Unitarian Universalist congregation is nearby; and the surrounding community is blessed with solid medical facilities, cultural and intellectual stimulation, and natural beauty. The Picketts have chosen a retirement village in Charlottesville, Virginia, home of the University of Virginia, nestled in the foothills of the Blue Ridge mountains, known for its relatively mild climate, and not too far away from any of their three daughters. Gene and Helen may wait until one or the other of them can no longer take care of their Cape Cod home, or they may simply migrate to Charlottesville when the time seems right.

Wintry Spirituality

Gene Pickett has always considered it a deficiency that his spiritual growth came through adversity, particularly within the Unitarian Universalist fold known for its upbeat, positive philosophy. After confessing that he identified with the company of religious pilgrims who embraced a "wintry spirituality," Pickett acknowledged in his 1984 General Assembly address that this avenue to growth was beneficial not only for himself but for countless other Unitarian Universalists. He willingly came out of the closet to advocate its relevance and value.

Pickett has never believed that adversity per se will strengthen or build character, but he has gained insights into the nature of reality chiefly through trial and travail. Most of Gene's accumulated wisdom has emerged from personal difficulties and existential anguish. By enduring grave, life-threatening emotional pain, Pickett has been able to empathize pastorally with others during their dark nights of the soul. He would concur with Auden's sentiment: "May I, composed like them of eros and dust, beleaguered by the same negation and despair, show an affirming flame."

Summery Unitarian Universalists find the myth of Sisyphus a depressing tale, since the struggle seems hopeless with the stone eternally rolling back down the hill. For Gene there is a subtle pleasure and meaning experienced in his life through the bold act of continually pushing stones up mountains. As an existentialist he has sought and uncovered his purpose amid the vicissitudes of daily existence. He has never anticipated a happy ending to this earthly trek. He is a thoroughgoing agnostic on the question of an afterlife. His basic philosophy of life is: "Whether or not God cares, I care. Whether or not the universe exudes meaning, we humans must!"

Gene additionally holds: "Our only certain human immortality is that of influence, and virtue is its own reward. Even immortality of influence is a rather weak reed, because it will last but a short while—perhaps with our immediate children and the institutions with which we have been involved, then our memory will fade quickly."

Although Gene experienced the absence of God throughout most of his life, he will neither affirm nor deny the presence of the divine working in the midst of human tragedy. He simply remains open to the possibility. In a succinct CLF radio spot, Pickett once phrased his view of divine involvement as follows: "I believe God works *through* us and not *for* us. We have to rely on ourselves and on our free minds to help us. The future is not irrevocably set. We have the capacity to rise to the demands of this life with all its complexities and uncertainties."

Pickett's copious sermon files reveal many variations on

the recurring theme of loneliness. At Christmas time he felt more comfortable preaching on the "darkest time of the year" than mouthing conventional references to the triumph of returning light. Yet he loved singing Christmas carols. Gene tells the following tale in one of his presidential "Pickett Lines": "It was over thirty Christmases ago that Helen and I had serious thoughts of marriage. As we discussed the possibility in a dingy little tavern near the seminary in Chicago, she expressed the real concern that if she married a Unitarian Universalist, she would have to give up Christmas and carol singing! And this she would miss very much. I assured her that if this was her major objection, we could get married tomorrow. She finally said yes, and that is why we have always sung many carols in the churches I have served."

Of course, it should be noted that Pickett's favorite holiday hymn has always been the somber, obscure "In the Lonely Midnight." But Gene is not a scrooge; he personally enjoys the celebratory aspects of the Christmas season. In fact, he still immerses himself in tree decorating and lavish gift buying, as his father did before him. He has never suffered from seasonal affective disorder, which can result from lack of sunlight during the winter months. Pickett's personality is simply grounded in the treasures and burdens of a wintry soil, regardless of the time of the year. Although he has always tended to run a low-grade depression, Gene considers himself future-oriented and hopeful, so his wintry temperament never assumes the guise of grimness. Melancholy is perhaps a more fitting term.

Gene is particularly fond of the following remarks by Donald Murray, *Boston Globe* columnist: "As a member of the 'have-a-good-day' society, I used to feel guilty when a mood of quiet sadness would pass over me. Not anymore. I've slowly come to discover that an occasional mild depression may be appropriate over sixty, even healthy.

"I have reasons for sadness as I think back, but there is no bitterness, no anger, surprisingly little regret, just a passing melancholy that gives these days I am still living a special texture and meaning.

"Over sixty, my favorite time of day is before sundown, when long shadows give rich texture to the fields and woods, and I remember the good life I have led, and appreciate, as I never could when I was young, the days I have left."

Reflections On Death

In Pickett's 1966 Easter address in Atlanta, Georgia, he expressed his fundamental seasonal theme: "Few of us stop to realize that the 'little deaths' we all experience are rehearsals for greater griefs and eventually for death itself. . . . In the end, the tragedy of death is not the dying, but rather dying without having ever fully lived. When life has been well lived, deeply lived, then when it is time to go, Freud is right, 'the goal of life is death.' To appreciate this is to understand death. And to understand death is to realize the joy and significance of life and this is to know one of the basic and ancient meanings of Easter."

In one of his "Pickett Lines" as UUA president, Gene revisited his readiness to embrace death: "To face this season whole or to appreciate the great mystery drama which is the Easter myth, we cannot overlook the fact of death, even in the midst of growth and life. To believe in the joy and triumph of life is not to banish death—it is to embrace it. To celebrate the return of the spring is not to deny the reality of death—it is to affirm the glory of life despite the presence of death. Anguish and joy, anxiety and delight, death of the body as well as the miracle of birth and growth—these are the warp and woof of the fabric of life.

"Death is one of the basic realities of our existence. It is a fact that we must live with and at last singly face and accept. Death comes to embrace us all. Since we cannot live forever, the 'here-and-now' should assume greater meaning. Our approaching death, whether abrupt or drawn out, is not the most important fact in our existence. The important aspect of ourselves is our life and what we make it mean."

Gene resonates more with Walt Whitman's "Come soothing death" than with Dylan Thomas's "Rage, rage against the dying of the light." He is willing to accept death rather than fight it, and wants to avoid the agonizingly, protracted death that his mother experienced. Consequently, he is strongly supportive of assisted suicide.

When suicides occurred during his parish ministries, Gene would invariably speak both to the particular loss and to the general topic. He viewed suicide not necessarily as an indication of debilitating mental illness, but sometimes as a justifiable and dignified way to complete one's earthly journey. Helen is sympathetic with Gene's views on assisted suicide, and since her father and his brothers all succumbed to Alzheimer's disease, she is fearful that she might fall prey to it as well.

She further reflects, "We have talked about assisted suicide and the possibility of a joint suicide pact. Maybe I can count on Gene to put me in the car and kill both of us with carbon monoxide. However, it would be easier for me to contemplate Gene's helping me commit suicide than for me to assist Gene." Nonetheless, since she knows how adamantly Gene feels about death with dignity, she would probably be motivated to help him carry out his wishes.

When Gene is asked what he would do if Helen died before him, he replies, "I wouldn't want to live on myself after Helen has died. Without her, the joy would ebb from the deepest places in my heart. I feel that overall I have had a good life, much better than I had any reason to expect. I have achieved things and been successful in areas that I never would have contemplated. Our life has become exceedingly, increasingly rich. When she dies, I would be ready to move on. She is what makes it all worthwhile now. I mean, we even share the Pickett House, with my name on it, and Helen has a room in that house with her name on it."

Helen phrases her views somewhat differently: "Each other is the best thing we have right now. The thing that would modify it for me would be the presence of the children and grandchildren, if I were still healthy." Gene would be ready to go when Helen dies. He is an unrepentant wintry spirit who, when the time is right, will willingly embrace death. Helen remains, in her own words, "a sobered yet summery soul."

Helen's preference is to have Gene bury her ashes under a tree especially planted in some churchyard or in one of her daughter's gardens. When pressed for particulars, Gene offers these thoughts on his own memorial service:

"Something simple, in the local church. An attractive flower arrangement, a string quartet playing, perhaps, Schubert's 'Death and the Maiden.' Some of my favorite readings, then concluding with Bloch's 'Kol Nidre' on the cello."

For Gene there is no single American city that he would call his home, yet when he and Helen visited Winfield recently, he was nostalgically touched by the lovely countryside and the sight of his old Methodist church with the nearby Pickett family graves. "Maybe, just maybe," Gene mused, "burying my ashes in the Ebenezer cemetery would be a way for me to go home again!"

At least he is intrigued by the thought.